Transboundary Game of Life

Masahiko Aoki

Transboundary Game of Life

Memoir of Masahiko Aoki

Springer

Masahiko Aoki
Stanford University
Stanford, CA, USA

Translated by Beth Cary, Oakland, CA, USA

ISBN 978-981-13-2756-8 ISBN 978-981-13-2757-5 (eBook)
https://doi.org/10.1007/978-981-13-2757-5

Library of Congress Control Number: 2018959254

This Springer imprint is published by the registered company Springer Nature Singapore Pte Ltd.
The registered company address is: 152 Beach Road, #21-01/04 Gateway East, Singapore 189721, Singapore

Foreword

Masahiko Aoki (1938–2015): His Pilgrimage and Legacies[1]

The man who never alters his opinion is like standing water,
and breeds reptiles of the mind.
William Blake, *The Marriage of Heaven and Hell*,
composed between 1790 and 1793.

It's more than a game. It's an institution.
Thomas Hughes, *Tom Brown's Schooldays*, 1857.

Masahiko Aoki passed away on July 15, 2015, at the age of 77, leaving all who knew him with a grave feeling of loss. Masa was an excellent scholar and an unforgettable person with the rare combination of a cool head and a warm heart. His brilliant and flamboyant life is marked by numerous academic distinctions and recognitions including the Nikkei Prize for Economic Book of the Year (1971) for *The Economic Theory of Organization and Planning*,[2] the election as a Fellow of the Econometric Society (1982), the Japan Academy Prize (1990) for *The Cooperative Game Theory of the Firm*[3] and *Information, Incentives, and Bargaining in the Japanese Economy*,[4] the Presidency of the Japanese Economic Association (1995–1996) and of the International Economic Association (2008–2011). However, his life was full of many upheavals and phoenix-like rebirths, as well as of multi-faceted academic accomplishments that left the clear mark of his original thinking and energetic leadership, which cannot be duly described by simply listing these ex-post honors. On this occasion of making his fascinating

[1]I delivered a speech at the *Masahiko Aoki Memorial Conference on Economics* held at the Bechtel Conference Center, Encina Hall, Stanford University on December 4, 2015. This foreword partly capitalizes on my Stanford speech. I am grateful to Kenneth Arrow, Nick Baigent, Kaushik Basu, Walter Bossert, Koichi Hamada, Takeo Hoshi, and Chikashi Moriguchi for their comments and useful information, which helped me greatly to write up this foreword.
[2]*Soshiki to Keikaku no Keizai-riron*, Tokyo: Iwanami Publishing Company, 1971.
[3]Oxford: Oxford University Press, 1984.
[4]Cambridge, UK: Cambridge University Press, 1988.

autobiography, originally published in Japanese, accessible to English readers, it is my great pleasure to put my personal recollections of Masa as a wonderful individual, as well as his academic and social legacies on record.

I met Masa in person for the first time at the beginning of the 1970s at a conference held in Japan. He was then in his early 30s and had already established himself as a dazzling scholar in mathematical economics with an international reputation. I was a young graduate student at Hitotsubashi University, and I served as an assigned discussant of his work on the informationally efficient and decentralized planning procedures for an economy with production externalities.[5,6] Being six years junior to him, I can personally testify to the fact that he exerted a magnetic influence on many young scholars in Japan.[7]

Even before this first personal encounter with Masa in the academic arena, I came to know of him around 1960 in a completely different circumstance. I was only a second-year high-school boy in the remote city of Nagoya, which is some 260 km beeline distance from Tokyo, and Masa was studying economics under the dogmatic influence of Marxism at the University of Tokyo. What made him famous nationwide, known even by a high-school boy in a distant city, was his active involvement in the National Federation of Students' Self-Government Association (*Zengakuren*), which was at the heart of the 1959–1960 intense campaign against the US–Japan Security Treaty that ran riot all over Japan.[8] As if to prepare for the 1959–1960 campaign, an organization called the Bund was formed in 1958, which played the leadership role in student activities that were not under the control of the Japanese Communist Party. Masa was one of the founding members of the Bund. When the new Japan–US Security Treaty was about to be signed, the student activists including the Bund members tried to prevent Prime Minister Nobusuke

[5]This work was subsequently published as Aoki, M., "Two Planning Processes for an Economy with Production Externalities," *International Economic Review*, Vol. 12, 1971.

[6]This first encounter with Masa eventually led to my move from the Department of Economics, Hitotsubashi University to the Kyoto Institute of Economic Research, Kyoto University as an Associate Professor, where I worked as his colleague for ten fruitful years specializing in social choice theory and welfare economics.

[7]A high proportion of graduate students majoring in economic theory at Kyoto University were under Masa's strong influence. I remember clearly one graduate seminar held at the beginning of the academic year, where about a dozen of graduate students introduced themselves by saying unanimously that they intend to pursue the theory of firms in comparative perspective, which was Masa's main research project around that time.

[8]The allied occupation of Japan after World War II was ended by the San Francisco Peace Treaty signed on September 8, 1951. The Security Treaty between the USA and Japan was signed the same day, which granted the USA the territorial means to establish in Japan a military presence in the Far East. Bilateral talks on revising the 1951 Security Treaty started in 1959, and the new Treaty of Mutual Cooperation and Security was signed on January 19, 1960, in Washington, DC. When the new treaty pact was submitted to the Japanese Diet for ratification, a fierce campaign against this pact was triggered. The leftist opposition was based on the fear that the new treaty might lead to the enduring subordination of Japan's independence under the US hegemony. Massive demonstrations and angry riots by students, trade union activists, and some ordinary citizens failed to prevent the passage of the new treaty pact, which was passed by default on June 19, 1960.

Kishi from flying to Washington, DC by force. Those who occupied Haneda Airport were arrested, and Masa was among 77 students who were detained for illegal trespass and property damage. Viewed from a distance, the young student leaders of the campaign seemed full of conviction in what they were doing and advocating. Although I had my intuitive doubts on the logic of their agitation and could not be too sympathetic to their extreme acts, I was fascinated by their dazzling resoluteness and wondered why they could sustain so much faith in their own campaign.

Being a second-year high-school boy, I was too naïve and ignorant of social sciences to identify the causes and consequences of my intuitive doubts about their acts and beliefs, and to establish my own stance vis-à-vis what was really at stake in the 1959–1960 movement. Nevertheless, this massive campaign and its aftermath made me wonder about the meaning and virtue of democratic methods of collective decision-making. Both sides of the dispute, the Liberal Democratic Party government and the leftist opposition, sent stern warnings on the imminent danger of the breakdown of democracy. However, the very fact that both sides were using the same portmanteau catchword of democracy sent me a clear signal that they were assigning very different meanings to one and the same term, viz. democracy. Although I could not crystallize at that time an operational definition of the democratic method of collective decision-making, it soon became clear to me that there are two distinct sides to the same coin, viz. the goodness of the final outcome to be brought about, and the intrinsic value of the decision-making procedure through which the final outcome is brought about. This naïve recognition persisted throughout my subsequent research activities in social choice theory and welfare economics. Later on, Masa and I had several heated discussions on this and related issues at the Kyoto Institute of Economic Research, Kyoto University.

The 1959–1960 campaign ended without accomplishing its proclaimed target, and the dejected activist students soon split into chaotic factions. Masa bade his farewell to the activist group altogether, and he went back to the study of economics at the University of Tokyo. As a matter of fact, not only did he leave the activist group, he also dissociated himself from Marxian economics, and proceeded anew to the study of orthodox neoclassical economics. What propelled him to this metamorphosis was his fated encounter with a marvelous article by Kenneth Arrow and Leonid Hurwicz.[9] In this epoch-making article, Arrow and Hurwicz showed that there is an isomorphism between their programming method for computing an optimal resource allocation and the idealized working of the perfectly competitive market mechanism. Thus, the decentralized market mechanism can bring about an optimal resource allocation under classical economic environments with universal convexity and without externalities, which the Central Planning Board (CPB) is

[9]Arrow, K. J. and L. Hurwicz, "Decentralization and Computation in Resource Allocation," in R. W. Pfouts, ed., *Essays in Economics and Econometrics*, Chapel Hill: University of North Carolina Press, 1960.

unable to accomplish due to the crucial fact that privately owned, and widely dispersed, information is beyond the reach of the CPB. Besides, there is no incentive on the part of private agents to comply voluntarily with the command of the CPB.

Masa recollects that by the time the 1960 uprising collapsed, he was completely fed up with the illogical, partisan, and political disputes in the leftist circles. This being the case, it struck him as a fresh revelation that Arrow and Hurwicz could pose fundamental questions of resource allocation and economic organizations and apply transparent logical methods for their precise analysis. This was exactly what Masa had been groping after. There is no wonder that he was intoxicated by this encounter with his destiny, which eventually led him to study at the Graduate School of the University of Minnesota, where he obtained his Ph.D. under the supervision of Leonid Hurwicz and John Chipman. Within a few years, he turned himself into a full-fledged scholar on the frontier of mathematical economic systems analysis with high distinction, which paved the road toward his highly reputable career at Stanford and Harvard, where he could nourish fruitful interactions with Kenneth Arrow and Janos Kornai.

It is not infrequent that Masa's conversion from Marxian economics to the frontier of neoclassical mathematical economics was misconstrued and criticized as if he betrayed his activist comrades and escaped to the USA for the sake of turning over a new leaf in orthodox academic circles. I dare to disagree with this cynical view for the sake of fairness. It is true that Masa's professional point of departure was to liberate himself from the influence of Marxian economics and proceed to the mathematical analysis of economic systems in the neoclassical tradition. In my perception, however, it is too shallow to regard Masa's Zengakuren-Bund experience as if it were a thwarted ambition in his youth, which is completely dead and buried in the past. Indeed, in his own recollection, the 1960 campaign was epoch-making in that it sent an unambiguous signal that the nature of the social game played in Japan was thereby altered beyond retrieval. On the one hand, it revealed that there is no future for a political system seeking a magic wand by supplementing the insufficient governability of the ruling political party by means of outright regulation, or by means of the police force or military power. On the other hand, it also revealed that the long-standing leftist myth of the "vanguard" who organizes and controls spontaneous political actions by ordinary citizens under its guidance is bankrupt beyond rectification. The upshot of this view is that the Bund played a Mephistopheles-like catalytic role as a switchman between two regimes, viz. the *militaristic and regulatory regime* and the *liberal democratic regime*.

There may still be some cynical criticism that Masa's later view is nothing but an ex-post rationalization of his past act of betrayal. My view is different. It reveals how deeply rooted is his lifetime concern with comparative institutions, and his early commitment to Marxian historical philosophy, as distinct from Marxian economics, was very much alive and kicking as an integral undercurrent of the evolution of his economics.

I should also mention the conspicuous versatility and impressive broadness of his research activities. Indeed, starting from the mathematical analysis of economic systems with strong emphasis on the decentralized planning procedure in non-classical economic environments, Masa's pilgrimage covered the game-theoretic analysis of firms, comparative institutional analysis, and the comparative institutional developments in East Asian economies. In my view, the most conspicuous feature of Masa's versatility and broadness of his research areas lies in the internal coherence of his analysis and the strong underlying aspiration that may be traced back even to his early interest in Marxian historical philosophy. In this sense, he was a bit more than an economic theorist; he was a unique social scientist with discipline and passion.

The nineteenth-century poet John Clare left in his letter to a friend the following memorable sentence: "Had Life a 2 edition—oh! how I wou'd correct it."[10] Being a bit of the perfectionist, Masa might have wanted to proofread and revise some minor details of his first life if he were provided with a chance of creating the second edition of his life. However, as Paul Samuelson observed in a conversation with me, which was conducted in a completely different context, "we should always attach importance to the first edition of anything."[11] In my judgment, there is no need for revising anything essential of Masa's life and work in view of his brilliant accomplishments in intellectual activities, his strong and warm ties with many friends and colleagues all over the world, and his vital and lasting influence on numerous fellow economists and young scholars. It is my belief that readers of this English version of Masa's Memoire would testify to the correctness of my personal judgment to this effect. It is also my belief that readers of this English version of Masa's Memoire will enjoy a unique experience and receive an abundance of material for fruitful thought for many years to come. Bon Voyage.

Tokyo, Japan
April 2018

Kotaro Suzumura
Professor Emeritus of Hitotsubashi University
Professor Emeritus and Honorary Fellow of Waseda University
Fellow of the Japan Academy

[10]This letter is kept in the British Library, Egerton Manuscript 2246, fol. 230v. I am indebted to Professor Nick Baigent of the London School of Economics, Mr. Robert Heyes, Honorary Membership Secretary of the John Clare Society, and Ms. Linda Curry, Former President of the John Clare Society, for tracking down the whereabouts and the precise wording of the cited sentence.

[11]This citation is taken from Suzumura, K., "An Interview with Paul Samuelson: Welfare Economics, 'Old' and 'New', and Social Choice Theory," *Social Choice and Welfare*, Vol. 25, 2005, p. 332.

Preface

This volume is an expanded version of "My Memoir" serialized in *Nihon Keizai Shimbun* newspaper during the month of October 2007. When I was approached by the newspaper about the serialization, my first reaction was one of hesitation. I had no confidence that I could spare the time when I had a pile of my academic work to complete. I was also concerned that being a "Memoir," I couldn't avoid giving an account of my student days, which I had never publicly spoken about, and I asked myself whether I was mentally prepared to do this. Ultimately, I agreed to the proposal as I was assured of two supporting factors.

One was that a sensitive reporter would prepare the text based on interviews with me; specifically, Yō Makino, who had prepared the text for Peter Drucker's "My Memoir" serialization, was chosen. As I had thought that among the many memoirs serialized in the newspaper, Drucker's was one of the most impressive, and my concerns were allayed.

The second factor was that around that time Prof. Hideo Ōtake of Kyoto University had published *Shinsayoku no Isan: New Left kara Post Modern e* (Heritage of the New Left: From the New Left to Post Modern) (University of Tokyo Press, 2007). This allowed me to think that the anti-Security Treaty struggle was becoming the subject of inquiry in the social sciences, lifting my feeling of it as a psychological burden.

I had thought to write about the intertwining of my own history and the larger history of the times. It was only toward the end of the serialization that I came to the realization that this endeavor, if I can overstate it, was actually related to my present struggles with theories of social science. Some of what I added toward the end of this book relates to this, but I think it is still in a preliminary state. However, there appears to be no easy solution to this study of mine, so I will let this stand as it is at this stage.

My collaboration with Yō Makino was extremely agreeable and productive. I asked him to schedule the interviews during Stanford University's summer vacation in August 2007. He was kind enough to arrange to come to Stanford for two weeks to interview me.

The newspaper's editorial department had chosen Makino because he had become familiar with American academics through interviewing Peter Drucker. As I began working with him, I discovered another reason that made our work truly collaborative. His father, a few years older than me, had been an activist in the student movement. We had friends in common between us, and this work was a chance for Makino to rediscover part of his family as well. Because of this, almost half of this memoir covers the time from my student movement days to when I graduated from activism and departed at age 26 for the USA to pursue academic studies, veering away from what I had initially anticipated.

Being the obsessive sort, I added and changed a considerable amount from the draft prepared from the interviews, making me responsible for the final content of the entire volume. I was fortunate to have had many people whom I have encountered in my life and who have been a great influence on me.

My wife Reiko has shared the greater part of my life as a scholar with me. She has been a wonderful partner, understanding of my work, compensated for my shortcomings, and has been a staunch supporter of six of my intellectual ventures. For this volume, she gave me advice on content as well as phrasing and offered careful editing of the text. Thank you.

Stanford, USA Masahiko Aoki
March 2008

Preface for the English Edition

Masahiko Aoki passed away on July 15, 2015, at the age of 77. Aoki, an economic theorist, made contributions to various fields including mechanism design, theory of the firm, corporate governance, Japanese economy, Chinese economy, economic history, and comparative institutional analysis, the field he created with his colleagues at Stanford University. He changed the way we approach national economies outside the USA and Europe, such as those of Japan and China. At the same time, he changed economic theory so that it can be applied to those economies.

When Masahiko Aoki started his research on the Japanese economy, the study of the Japanese or the Chinese economic system had little overlap with mainstream economic theory. Many scholars argued that characteristics that differentiated those economies from the USA and Western European ones are explained only by the unique culture of Asia. The standard economic theory also lacked the proper tools to understand those economies that appear different from market-based capitalist economies in the West. Masahiko Aoki filled this gap by seriously applying standard tools in economics to understand the Japanese economic system. At the same time, Aoki also advanced economic theory to explain why we observe seemingly different economic systems in different places and times and how an economic system evolves over time.

This book is the English version of the *Memoir of Masahiko Aoki* that was published in Japanese in 2008 (青木昌彦『私の履歴書 人生越境ゲーム』日本経済新聞出版社, Masahiko Aoki, *Watashi no Rirekisho: Jinsei Ekkyō Game*, Nihon Keizai Shimbun Shuppan-sha). In this memoir, Aoki goes over his life as a young boy in Japan immediately after WWII, as an activist who opposed rearmament of Japan under the US–Japan Security Alliance, as a student of Marxist economics first and then modern mathematical economics, and eventually as a leading economist in both Japan and the USA. He looks back on his graduate student days at Minnesota, and the experiences as a young and rising economist at Stanford, Harvard, and Kyoto. The book reveals the motivations for Aoki's major contributions to economics, including analysis of the Japanese economy and development of comparative institutional analysis. The book also describes Aoki's efforts to build several research institutions including the Stanford Japan Center, the Research

Institute of Economy, Trade, and Industry (RIETI), the Virtual Center for Advanced Studies in Institution (VCASI), and the Center for Industrial Development and Environmental Governance (CIDEG).

Aoki likens his life to a game, which is an analytical concept that he often used in academic research. For example, he characterized the corporate organization as the equilibrium of a game between management and workers. His Comparative Institutional Analysis (CIA) explains an economic system as a set of equilibria of many games in various aspects and levels of economic, social, and political interactions. Aoki says his game of life has been "transboundary" in two senses. He lived and conducted research in two countries: Japan and the USA. He also visited China numerous times and studied its economy. In addition to crossing the boundaries in the geographical sense, Aoki also moved between many fields in economics and often ventured outside economics into history, sociology, psychology, and political science.

Until now, his memoir was available only in Japanese and in Chinese. I hope this English edition will allow young social scientists everywhere to touch the life and work of Masahiko Aoki and be inspired to make their own versions of a "transboundary game of life."

I was not a student of Masa Aoki in a narrow sense, but I learned tremendously from his written work as well as from talking with him. I feel lucky that I was a colleague of his for the last three years of his life. I am very honored to have worked on the project to publish this English edition of his memoir.

The translation from the Japanese version was conducted by Beth Cary, who also worked with Masa on some projects and is familiar with his writing. Throughout the book, references to people's positions, organizations, etc., are as of the writing of the Memoir (2007 for the parts published in the newspaper series or 2008 for the parts added when the book came out), unless otherwise noted. For the titles of Japanese books cited in the Memoir, the English title is given when an English translation exists. If no English translation is found, the Japanese title is spelled in Romanization with English translation in parentheses. When a person's name is mentioned for the first time, the given name (e.g., Prime Minister Jun'ichirō Koizumi) is shown even when the Japanese version only refers to the surname.

I thank Reiko Aoki and her daughters Maki and Kyoko who encouraged me to embark on this project. Professor Kōtarō Suzumura, who is a great economist himself and a longtime friend of Masa, wrote the superb Foreword that only he could write. I give him my deep thanks. I also thank Meiko Kotani at the Japan Program at the Asia Pacific Research Center (APARC) at Stanford University for providing administrative assistance including scanning the pictures for this book.

Financial support for the project was provided by the Japan Fund at the Freeman Spogli Institute for International Affairs (FSI) and the Japan Program at APARC, both at Stanford University. Finally, I am grateful to Juno Kawakami at Springer, who understood the value of this project and guided it to completion. Without her efforts and patience, this project would not have materialized.

March 2018 Takeo Hoshi

Contents

About the Author

Masahiko Aoki was the Henri and Tomoye Takahashi Professor Emeritus of Japanese Studies in the Department of Economics, and a senior fellow of the Stanford Institute of Economic Policy Research and the Freeman Spogli Institute for International Studies at Stanford University.

Aoki was a theoretical and applied economist with a strong interest in institutional and comparative issues. He specialized in the theory of institutions, corporate architecture and governance, and the Japanese and Chinese economies.

His most recent book, *Corporations in Evolving Diversity: Cognition, Governance, and Institutions*, based on his 2008 Clarendon Lectures, was published in 2010 by Oxford University Press. It identifies a variety of corporate architecture as diverse associational cognitive systems and discusses their implications to corporate governance, as well their modes of interactions with society, polity, and financial markets within a unified game-theoretic perspective. His previous book, *Toward a Comparative Institutional Analysis*, was published in 2001 by MIT Press. This work developed a conceptual and analytical framework for integrating comparative studies of institutions in economics and other social science disciplines using game-theoretic language. Aoki's research has been also published in the leading journals in economics, including the *American Economic Review, Econometrica*, the *Quarterly Journal of Economics, Review of Economic Studies*, the *Journal of Economic Literature, Industrial and Corporate Change*, and the *Journal of Economic Behavior and Organizations.*

Aoki was the president of the International Economic Association from 2008 to 2011 and was also a former president of the Japanese Economic Association. He was a fellow of the Econometric Society and the founding editor of the *Journal of Japanese and International Economies*. He was awarded the Japan Academy Prize in 1990, and the sixth International Schumpeter Prize in 1998. Between 2001 and 2004, Aoki served as the president and chief research officer of the Research Institute of Economy, Trade, and Industry, an independent administrative institution specializing in public policy research in Japan.

Aoki graduated from the University of Tokyo with a B.A. and an M.A. in economics and earned a Ph.D. in economics from the University of Minnesota in 1967. He was formerly an assistant professor at Stanford University and Harvard University and served as both an associate and full professor at the University of Kyoto before rejoining the Stanford faculty in 1984.

Printed with permission from https://aparc.fsi.stanford.edu/people/masahiko_aoki

Chapter 1
Seven Intellectual Ventures

In August 2005, nearly fifty years after I set my mind to aspire to become an economist, I headed for Marrakesh, Morocco, to attend the International Economic Association World Congress.[1] When I arrived at the hotel, who should walk toward me but then President of the Association, Professor Janos Kornai, and his wife. He greeted me with the words, "I have good news! You've been selected President by the executive committee." He added, "You won by just one vote."

At the following World Congress to be held in June 2008 in Istanbul, I would be formally appointed President of the International Economic Association for a three-year term. Eminent economists such as Paul Samuelson, Kenneth Arrow, and Amartya Sen had previously held that position. The main task of the President is to organize the program for the World Congress held every three years; and I thought this might allow me to make some waves in the future course of economics.

In the normal progression of events, a scholar's life is far from a stormy one; and, during my high school years when I began to think in vague terms of becoming a scholar, I had no way of predicting the fluctuations that would later come in my life. In my case, however, there was a time when I was placed in solitary confinement at Sugamo Prison for my enthusiasm for the radical student movement of my university days, and, as a result, I later received notification of deportation from the United States where I had gone for further study. I had buried these events deep in my subconscious. But now that I have the chance to look back on the course of my life, it seems to me that a single thread carries through to this day.

My specialization is economics. The starting point for my professional life was mathematical analysis of economic systems after I had cast off the Marxist influence of my university student days. Eventually, I became dissatisfied with such analysis, and attempted to cultivate the field of comparative institutional analysis. This field of

---

[1] The International Economic Association (IEA) was organized as a nongovernmental organization in 1950 at the urging of UNESCO. It is a federation of associations representing economists in various nations, with over sixty member associations. The Japanese association is the Science Council of Japan. See http://www.iea-world.org.

M. Aoki, *Transboundary Game of Life*,
https://doi.org/10.1007/978-981-13-2757-5_1

study considers how institutional frameworks composed of economic and political institutions, combined with social norms and culture, can be diverse in their constituted "forms"; and, further, seeks out the unified principles that lie as the base of these diverse forms.

Looking back, social studies was my favorite subject in my childhood. Accumulating various experiences and observing many different societies no doubt gradually led me to develop a framework for my thoughts. This process has been imbued with my experiences as a student activist and the lessons I learned as a mathematical economist.

Since my departure to study abroad in the U.S. in 1964, I have continued a life of going back and forth between Japan and foreign countries. When I think about it, I have spent about half the time since then abroad. I have often crossed the boundaries between East and West; and within the East between Japan and China. This has been invaluable in gaining insights and knowledge useful to understand societal structures. In particular, for the field of social sciences, which does not allow experiments at the macro level, the knowledge gained by comparative observation helps to avoid arbitrary viewpoints in formulating theories. Observing other countries also allows us to realize the importance of things we overlook as taken for granted in our own country. A similar viewpoint has been expressed in a literary manner by the comparative sociologist Benedict Anderson when he stated, "I felt a kind of vertigo. For the first time in my young life I had been invited to see my Europe as through an inverted telescope."[2]

Having said this, I have come to realize more and more that crossing the boundaries of academic disciplines is not an easy matter. This is why it might feel like "vertigo." It is because we start to see that the institutional organizations of society are constituted not only from visible "forms" such as statutes, but also in large part by what might be called a subconscious held in common by the people in that society.

I heard an affecting episode told by the eminent psychiatrist and psychotherapist Carl Jung from his disciple, the late, lamented cultural psychologist Hayao Kawai.[3] When Jung's friend, a long-time missionary to China who had translated the *I Ching* and had become thoroughly acclimated to Chinese culture, returned to his country, he reverted to being a regular European. Jung felt a deep apprehension about the loss of his friend's important mission to transfer the wisdom of the East to the West. Just as he had feared, his friend fell into a deep psychologically disturbed state and died. Jung concluded that understanding two different cultures in an integrated way while being caught between the two entails this sort of extreme psychological danger.

As to myself, I find it not too difficult to write articles in English in my specialty, but in every day conversation, whether in English or in Japanese, at times I falter and my words are not understandable or grammatically correct. This makes me particularly susceptible to agreeing with Jung's interpretation. Going back and forth

---

[2] Anderson, Benedict. *The Spectre of Comparisons: Nationalism, Southeast Asia and the World*, Verso: 1998; p. 2.

[3] Kawai, Hayao. *Yungu shinrigaku nyūmon* (Introduction to Jungian Psychology), Baifūkan: 1967; pp. 296–298.

between two worlds is an invaluable experience for a social scientist, but there is no doubt that experiencing another country's culture and institutions and facing those head on bring on conflicts in one's subconscious. It may be easier to deny one's experiences in the foreign country and regress into extolling one's own country, or, conversely, to curry favor with foreigners and find fault with the ways of one's own country. Neither does it seem to me to be as simple as adding up the ways of life of the West and Japan and dividing them in two.

It was not only geographically that I crossed boundaries. As I stated at the outset, I had begun to consider becoming a scholar from my days in high school. That path, however, was not a straight one. At times I crossed the boundaries of the world of scholarship, while at other times I endeavored to cross the boundaries of traditional academic disciplines. Not content with merely thinking about ways in which societies were organized and their differences, I attempted to challenge the ways of thinking and customary practices considered a matter of course in the world—the rules of societal games, as it were. To this end, I have been involved in the creation of seven "ventures" in Japan and abroad. The word "venture" is defined as a business or undertaking whose result is uncertain. What I have been involved in are all undertakings of institution-building related to ideas, research, and education, whose only investment has been intellectual capital. Of those, some have ended in failure, others have developed smoothly to the point that I have let them go, and still others are those whose results are unknown quantities.

My venturing spirit—in cynical terms, being rash or scatterbrained—came from the DNA I inherited from my ancestors; but it was also induced and propelled by my engagement with the times and the international arena. It may not have been "stumbling seven times and rising eight times" as in the old Japanese phrase, but my life and academic course have been obstinate repetitions of "commitment to a new undertaking → sense of accomplishment at success, or withdrawal due to setbacks → reset." Figuratively speaking, one could say I have been challenging myself to a life-long "trans-boundary" game with no resolution. During this time, I have encountered, been helped by, and learned from many people, both in Japan and abroad. I wish to set down the path I have taken as it relates to the changes in the times I have lived.

Let me start by relating the activities of my student movement days, whose setback was what prompted the germination of my current self.

Chapter 2
Student Movement

January 1960, I sat inside the police station at Manseibashi in Akihabara, Tokyo. Kandagawa River flowed below the steep embankment, and frigid air blew upward. I was thrown into the holding cell with a seasoned warehouse burglar, who intimidated the warden; and my interrogation was not by a gentle-seeming officer in charge of ideological offenses (Metropolitan Police Agency Public Security Section 2), but by a brawny detective in charge of labor movements (Public Security Section 1). It was a time when police were activated during intense confrontations between labor and management. His attitude was so overbearing that my mother, who had brought me a care package, was turned away, for the reason that my identity was unknown as I was refusing to answer any questions.

What was interesting to me was that it was not the warden who took charge of the various suspects in the holding cell and maintained order, but rather the job of the head prisoner in the same cell block. When he learned of the circumstances of my arrest from sneaking a peek at the newspaper in the interrogation room, he became sympathetic to my plight and tried to give me a higher status in the cell. And the warden, knowing that I was a student at University of Tokyo, asked my advice, "What should I do to get my son accepted at Tokyo University?" I love to eat, and was quite satisfied with the prison supper of barley rice, pickled daikon radish, with some dried *hijiki* seaweed sprinkled on top. Even now, when I eat *hijiki*, I am reminded of those days, though not quite to the extent of Proust's madeleine.

I was arrested when, along with a large number of students, I erected a barricade at Haneda Airport to try to prevent Prime Minister Nobusuke Kishi from departing to visit the United States. The Prime Minister's purpose in visiting the U.S. was to sign the revised U.S.-Japan Security Treaty; this Security Treaty was about to become the focus of the largest-scale student movement in Japan's history.[1] The student

[1]Record of my days of anti-U.S.-Japan Security Treaty struggles are detailed in: "60nen Anpo, sono gekidō no kiseki": http://www.ne.jp/asahi/karanohako/m.t/kiroku-anpo2.html; http://www.ne.jp/asahi/karanohako/m.t/kiroku-anpo3.html; http://www.ne.jp/asahi/karanohako/m.t/kiroku-anpo4.html.

M. Aoki, *Transboundary Game of Life*,
https://doi.org/10.1007/978-981-13-2757-5_2

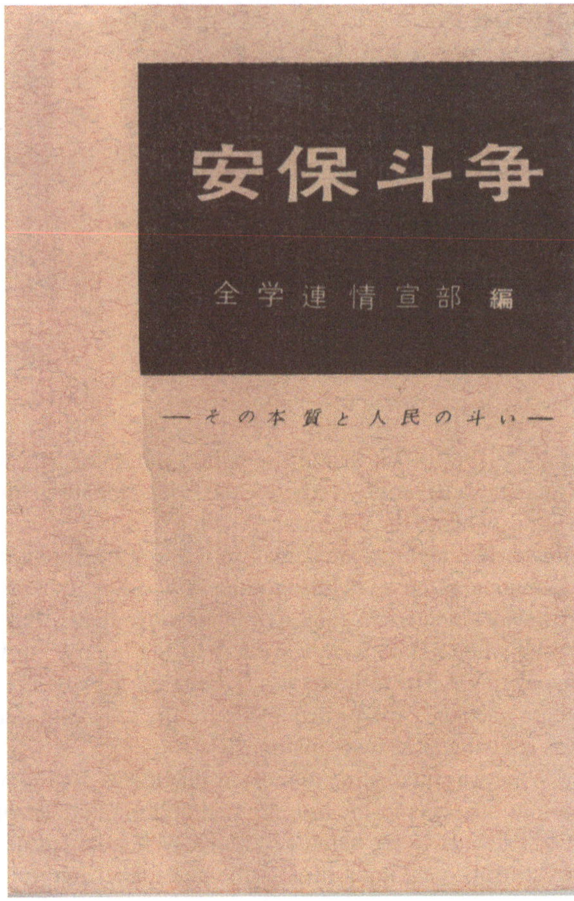

Fig. 2.1 Cover of "Anpo Tōsō" (Anti-Security Treaty Struggle), edited by Information Propaganda Section, Zengakuren, July 1959

movement was organized by the Zengakuren (All-Japan Federation of Student Self-Government) comprising practically all of the student self-governments of the nation's major universities. And it was an organization called the Bund (communists' collective), created just a year or so earlier, that was the core that promoted the activities of the Zengakuren. I was the information propaganda director of the Zengakuren and also one of the founding members of the Bund (Fig. 2.1).

The established leftist political movement, made up of the General Council of Trade Unions, Socialist Party, and Communist Party, saw the revision of the U.S.-Japan Security Treaty as a movement that would make Japan even more subordinate to the U.S. As these groups were under the overwhelming dominance of the Communist bloc led by the Soviet Union, they thought as a matter of course that the greatest enemy of the Soviet Union, the U.S., was their enemy as well. But the Zengakuren considered the Security Treaty revision to be a military alliance that would resurrect the imperialistic ambitions of Japan's political leaders. If we peel away the characteristic leftist rhetoric, I think we can say that the perspective of the Zengakuren was closer to a true understanding of history. This was because the Bund was an independent organization that thought things through on its own.

We learned on the day before that Prime Minister Kishi had changed his schedule to secretly depart from Haneda Airport in the early morning of January 16, in order to evade the protest movement. By 8 p.m., nearly one thousand activists had entered the airport, and after the airport was closed several thousand more gathered outside. Within the airport, we formed a barricade of tables and chairs on the stairs leading to the departure lobby to prepare for the onslaught by the police and stood our ground in the restaurant. The idea must have been to rush out to the runway in guerilla fashion once the departure time arrived, but this was no way to stop the Prime Minister from visiting the U.S. In the event, the fully prepared police battalion broke through our barricade, pulled us out one by one, identified us, and arrested all of the leaders of the Zengakuren and Bund. The total number arrested was 77, and I was one of them. The charge was illegal entry into a building and destruction of items, which was akin to those often brought against organized crime groups. One could say this was a self-inflicted botched tactic that left no way out, but this incident indicated the rise of the Bund as a player that could not be ignored under the increasingly strained political conditions.

Meanwhile, Prime Minister Kishi headed for the airport from his official residence along the Tama River and across the bridge escorted by ten police motorcycles and four trucks filled with 260 policemen. Apparently, some 70 mass media vehicles followed them. The method of this departure, practically running off under the cover of night, can be said to have cast doubts about the validity of the purpose of the visit to the U.S., which should have been Kishi's major moment on the world stage.

The Bund was formed in December 1958. A few dozen members from the Zengakuren leadership and the "cells" of major universities, such as University of Tokyo, Kyoto University, Hokkaido University, Kyushu University, and Waseda University, gathered at the initial meeting held at Medical Dental Pharmaceutical Hall in Hongō. The cells were the smallest units of the Communist Party of Japan, and I was an unofficial member of the University of Tokyo cell. Although I was only twenty years old, I presented an ambitious report titled "Review of International Communist Movements" criticizing Soviet and Japanese Communist Parties.[2] Shigeo Shima proposed the formation of an independent revolutionary organization, which was unanimously accepted. I became one of the five members of the secretariat. And at the Zengakuren general meeting held the following day, I became the information propaganda director. There were undercurrents of intense struggles regarding how to proceed with our movement, as I will mention later, but at this meeting, the student movement, which had long been under the control of the Communist Party, parted ways with the party.[3]

---

[2]"Puroretaria tsūshin: No. 6" (Proletarian bulletin), December 10, 1960; in Shima, Shigeo (supervising ed.), *Bunto no shisō* 4 (Ideology of the Bund) (Hihyōsha: 1992).

[3]Circumstances about those days are detailed in Shima, Shigeo, "Bunto Shishi (Zenhen)" (Personal history of the Bund (volume one), in Shima, Shigeo (supervising ed.), *Bunto no shisō* 1 (Ideology of the Bund) (Hihyōsha: 1992).

As to the naming of the organization, we didn't have any concrete image or manifesto other than our intention to form a radical movement separate from the Communist Party, and it seemed presumptuous to call ourselves a party. As I was entrenched in Marxist history, I came up with the idea of borrowing the mid-nineteenth century name of "Marxist Alliance." This alliance was no more than an assortment of multifarious "revolutionaries," "activists," and "conspirators" which did not have much impact on the 1848 "revolution." Yet, that period was the background for the young Marx, who had a good reputation as a theorist, to be commissioned to write, although belatedly, a manifesto, which became the "Communist Manifesto," whose ideology greatly influenced the entire world for over a century. "Alliance" in German is "Bund," and it became our name as it seemed fresher to us than the exclusionist, dark image of "Partei," or "Party."

This was my first intellectual venture.

Chapter 3
Three Influential Seniors

After the Haneda Airport incident, the mass media heaped all sorts of abuse on the student activists of the Zengakuren and Bund, calling us "gangster student activists" (Asahi Shimbun newspaper), "political bike gang" (Shūkan Asahi weekly), and "central staff of academic-cap revolution" (Shūkan Yomiuri weekly). Since by that time there were no activists who were boorish enough to still be wearing the four-cornered academic caps, this was a laughable anachronism. The Chair of the Zengakuren, Kentarō Karōji, was a witty dandy, who was in ecstasy, ordering a biker gang-style leather jacket stitched with the word "red lightning" on the back.

I happened to join up with Karōji and the others, but it was not my classes in university but rather the intellectual stimulation I received from three men who were a few years my senior who were the overwhelming driving force influencing me.

When I entered University of Tokyo (Fig. 3.1), I had wanted to become a historian. I began to participate in the History Research Society which had an office in the clock tower building on the Komaba campus. This was a time when Marxism still held sway over intellectuals and students, and the status of the study of history was its focal point. Among the group's members were several who became renowned in the fields of modern economic history and political history, such as Naosuke Takamura, Junji Banno, and Taichirō Mitani. One such person was one of my seniors who still exuded the atmosphere of the square academic-cap days: lean, long-haired, and hugely charismatic. He was expelled from high school in 1950, during the anti-red purge student movement. He was accepted at University of Tokyo after taking the university qualifying exam (rather than the usual university entrance exam); later, as professor of philosophy at Nagoya University and at University of Tokyo, he had a great influence on students during the Zenkyōtō (National Federation of All Campus) student movement in the late 1960s. This was Wataru Hiromatsu.

Early on, he invited me to coffee at the Student Union. I was suspicious, so I asked him why. He told me, "The Communist Party is no good anymore, but we're going to resurrect real Marxism in the University of Tokyo cell. Will you participate in this?" He must have noticed me as, from the start of my university days, I had been selected to become class representative and had made assertive statements about political

M. Aoki, *Transboundary Game of Life*,
https://doi.org/10.1007/978-981-13-2757-5_3

Fig. 3.1 Entering university, with my mother

activism in debates at the class rep meetings of student self-government, and at the History Research Group. I was surprised that organizations like cells, which I had only read about in newspapers and books, actually existed around me. But being only eighteen years old, and a rather carefree sort, my spirit of adventure was aroused and I thought it might be fun to join. Hiromatsu later pulled away from the movement to focus on academics, so I didn't have much contact with him. But as this was an encounter that set my course in life, I recall it very clearly.

By 1956, the student movement was once again on a rising tide. The Japanese Communist Party had engaged in self-criticism concerning its armed struggle of the first half of the 1950s, and was attempting to bring to students the soft line from the Soviet Union, consisting of "song and dance." But many of the old-hand student Party members were aiming for a more serious mass political struggle. A generational shift was occurring in which the "postwar" era was ending, and the concocted myth of "the only progressive party without responsibility for the war" no longer mattered.

When I joined the University of Tokyo cell, I saw that it was a gathering of glittering stars consisting of brilliant, exceptional, unique, and devilishly gifted talents. Among them was Kōji Ikuta, who followed the same life path as I until his untimely early death. He was rumored to have been in the secret military organization of the Communist Party, but by this time he held a leadership role in the fight between the mass struggle organization and the Communist Party headquarters. His characteristic way of pushing his glasses up as they slid down his nose and persuading people by his faltering speech made everyone trust in him.[1]

[1]Until just before I entered University of Tokyo at the Komaba campus, Ikuta had been living in the Social Science Research Group (Shaken) room at Komaba dormitory. In the same room was Ken'ichi Kōyama, who later became Chair of the Zengakuren (All-Japan Federation of Student

At Ikuta's urging, I went to meet Hidemitsu Saeki, then a graduate student in mathematics who lived in Yokohama. He lived in his family's Buddhist temple. Under the pen name Ichiri Yamaguchi, Saeki wrote sensational articles for the University of Tokyo cell bulletin, and was considered a divine presence by activists.[2] He stated that the problem with Japan's leftist movement is not only caused by the Japanese Communist Party, but was also because the Soviet Union, the central body, had betrayed the original communist movement. The scales fell from my eyes, as I felt that I had seen the light.

We spoke to each other about Trotsky in the dimness of the temple priest's quarters. Although Trotsky was one of the leaders of the Russian Revolution, he was ousted by his political foe Stalin and assassinated in Mexico. Years later, when I was invited to speak at a university in Mexico, I had the chance to see the house where Trotsky was killed. It was surrounded by a high wall, and there were remains of bullet holes here and there that had been shot from an automobile by the artist Siqueiros among the Stalinists who attempted to assassinate him. In the end, Trotsky was killed by a mountaineering ice-axe to his head wielded by an assassin sent by Stalin pretending to be a Trotskyite. The study where this took place remains as it was on that day. In the garden were rabbits said to be the descendants of those kept by Trotsky himself.

Saeki's articles were actually based on Trotsky's writings. Although we learned about the mistakes of international communism from his writings, we did not succumb to the persistent calling to join the Fourth International (the international organization founded by Trotsky in resistance to Stalin) by Trotsky's followers. This caused us to be attacked on practically a daily basis in sweeping generalizations as "Trotskyite subversive elements" by *Akahata*, the Communist Party's organ.[3]

It is true that Trotsky was a gifted revolutionary, and after his exile was a first-class writer, but his political influence had already waned. Yet the Fourth International was using a bizarre tactic of burrowing inside the organization by using a "joining tactic" by communist parties and socialist parties. But we no longer held any illusion that we could change the Communist Party from within, and were prepared to go our own way. We thought that "revolutionary internationalism" was not going to

Self-Government). The atmosphere of the student life and how the leftist students lived, and Ikuta's personality, are vividly described in the remembrances of the dormitory residents of the time. Koga, Yasumasa (ed.) "1994 Tōdai Komabaryō Shaken" (1994 University of Tokyo Komaba Dormitory Social Science Research Group).

[2]Yamaguchi, Ichiri. "Jūgatsu kakumei no michi to wareware no michi: kokusai kyōsanshugi undō no rekishiteki kyōkun" (The road of the October Revolution and our road: historical lessons from the international communist movement), Nihon Kyōsantō Tōdai Saibō Kikanshi: *Marukusu Rēnin shugi*, dai 9 gō, (Japan Communist Party University of Tokyo Cell Bulletin: Marxism-Leninism, No. 9), January 1958.

[3]For example, the day after the November 27, 1959 storming of the Diet building, the Japan Communist Party issued an extra edition and stated, "The majority of the leadership of the Zengakuren is Trotskyite, a provocateur group conspiring to infiltrate the democratic movement." It also stated, "We must fight to expel from the democratic camp the Trotskyite group that preys on the Communist Federation and Socialist Student Federation regardless of whether they are students or not." This sort of non-rational attack was persistently repeated on a daily basis throughout the anti-Security Treaty struggle.

be accomplished by making our aim that of joining the Fourth International, which was gasping its last breath, or by engaging in anti-U.S. struggles as hand maiden to the national interests and party interests of the Soviet Union or China. Rather, we aimed to generate a movement with international impact in our own nation. While I no longer use the modifier "revolutionary," I think even now that this is what true internationalism is.

Shortly after having made a legendary impact, Saeki went to study mathematics abroad in Poland, in the communist sphere, under the auspices of the international student federation organization. This was most likely due to the consideration of Ikuta and others who thought it was too much of a waste of the talents of such a brilliant mind as Saeki's to remain working on day-to-day party struggles. I heard that Saeki listened to the Security Treaty protest struggles glued to a shortwave radio in his lodgings in far-off Eastern Europe. He never returned to Japan, but instead went to Canada and became a professor of mathematics there.

With such surroundings at University of Tokyo, there was no lack of high-grade intellectual stimulation from people who were my seniors and classmates. While I diligently attended classes in my first semester at university, after that I only went to class when I needed to be at discussion sessions, and spent my time reading books like *Das Kapital* and *The Collected Works of Marx and Engels*. By my second year, I was busy going back and forth between the Komaba dormitory, which I had snuck into illegally, and the self-government office and the History Research Group room. In the morning, I took on the resented job of waking up the students asleep in the History Research room in the dormitory to round them up to pass out leaflets to the students commuting to campus at the Tōdaimae station. I also recruited any student I thought would be a good activist to the Bund. Among them are those who became renowned scholars or successful in business or the mass media. It was a time when the magma of the anti-Security Treaty movement was quietly being amassed.

By the time of my third year, when I would attend classes at the Hongō campus, I came to think that studying economics would be more in line with Marxism than studying history, and I decided to change my course of study to economics. Transferring from the Faculty of Letters, Department 2 (in those days) to the Faculty of Economics required having decent grades. It was amazing that I could do that, not having attended many classes. I can't divulge what happened too freely, but I did have the help of classmates. As I was thrown into such a chaotic situation, I was envious of my classmates who had no lack of time to attend classes, read books, and enjoy themselves in a normal fashion. But it wasn't long before I was given a lot of time to read books due to circumstances I could not have foreseen.

Chapter 4
Reiji Himeoka

When I return to Kyoto, where I lived for over fifteen years, I occasionally enjoy going for drinks with friends who used to be my “comrades” in their days of student activism at Kyoto University and are now active in business circles. On one of these occasions, the calligrapher Kyūyō Ishikawa was asked by some geishas in a Gion restaurant to write something with a brush. Being a fan of his calligraphic style, I asked him to write something on the paper coaster of my whiskey and water drink. As everyone held their breath wondering what would come out from his unique style with the brush, I saw the words “Reiji Himeoka.” Among such close friends, I am still known as Himeoka (Fig. 4.1).

When I began writing tracts in preparation for establishing the Bund, I followed the time-honored convention of old leftists and thought up a pen name. As I flipped through a telephone book, I think at the Zengakuren office or somewhere, the name Himeoka, someone who was in business in Taitō Ward, caught my eye. It was an

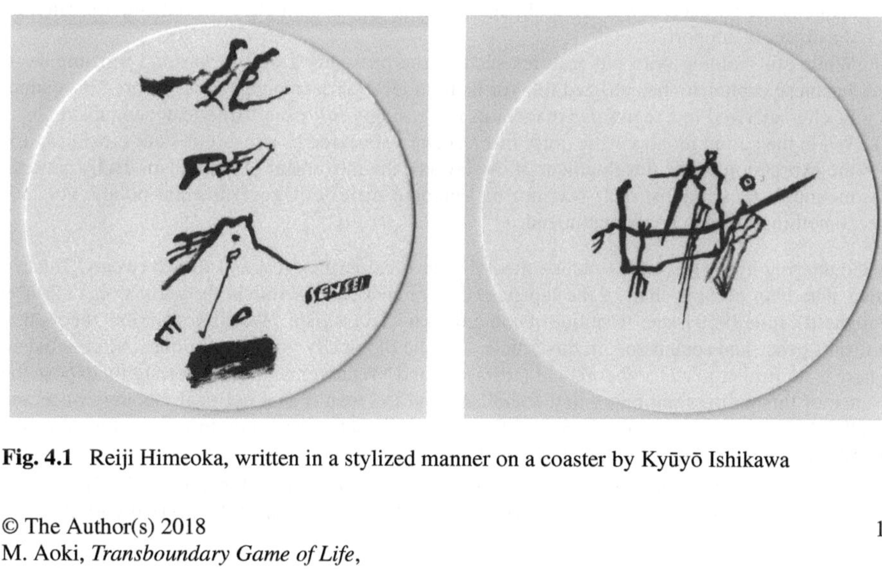

Fig. 4.1 Reiji Himeoka, written in a stylized manner on a coaster by Kyūyō Ishikawa

M. Aoki, *Transboundary Game of Life*,
https://doi.org/10.1007/978-981-13-2757-5_4

unusual surname, so I decided to borrow it. For the given name, I chose "Rei" from the syllable for Lenin, and "ji" from my close friend from middle school days on, Yūji Takahashi. I was teased by Minoru Morita, my senior in the Zengakuren and now a political analyst, that "the name brings to mind a singularly handsome youth," but that was not my intention.

Incidentally, my wife's name is Reiko, written in hiragana characters. Her parents named her Reiko with the same character I used for Reiji, but due to the official restrictions on the characters used to register names, they couldn't use it. I think this must be some sort of fate.

From before we started the Bund, I had been feverishly writing pieces on smashing the progressive myths related to previous communist movements, criticism about the Fourth International, and critiques of the dominant political economic analyses of Japan concerning leftist and labor movements.[1] They appeared mainly in the mimeographed "Proletarian Bulletin" before the start of the Bund and in printed form in "Communism" after the Bund was founded. There are now reprints of these publications priced at over $50,[2] but the copies of those publications and leaflets that I had stored in an apple crate were burned as trash by my mother while I was studying in the U.S. The year of the anti-Security Treaty struggles, I was asked by a publisher of new leftist works and wrote "The Establishment of Japan's State Monopolistic Capitalism" (Gendai Shichōsha). My political perspective changed afterward, and I was embarrassed at the naiveté of my level of understanding of economics, so I have not looked at that book since. In preparing this Memoir, I searched through my works

[1]My main targets of argument were the orthodox faction of the communist party under the leadership of the Soviet Union (including the mainstream of the Japan Communist Party), the structural reformist faction of the communist party (under the influence of the Italian Communist Party), and the Fourth International. The salient points of my argument were as follows.

(1) As the Soviet Union has transformed into a nation that maintains the special authoritarian status of the bureaucracy, it cannot be the leader of the revolutionary movement, nor can it be the object of support.
(2) While still holding onto old features such as the peasantry from prewar and wartime days, Japanese capitalism has utilized this for its high level of development. Therefore, this cannot be characterized in a regressive manner as increasingly following American capitalism.
(3) While the strong monopolistic corporate structure appeared as a result of state subsidies, it is the expression of the development of the laws of the movement of capitalism itself (national monopolistic capitalism). It was not an outcome merely of governmental policy, nor is it something that can be democratized.

Countering this series of "Himeoka theory" that I had written just as I turned twenty, Tetsuzō Fuwa, who later became chair of the Japanese Communist Party, wrote in the party's organ Zen'ei (Vanguard), June 1959 issue, "Critique of contemporary Trotskyism: 'World Revolution' theory that confronts peace and socialism." In this article, after he illogically vilified my points, he concluded, "There is no further need for theoretical criticism," and "What remains is to thoroughly expose the essence of this anti-revolutionary anti-socialism, and to crush it as a political ideology once and for all." With the dissolution of the Soviet Union some twenty years later, Fuwa was forced to say something along the lines of (1); and eventually keep silent about (2).

[2]Shima, Shigeo (supervising ed.), Takazawa, Kōji (ed.) *Bunto no shisō* (Ideology of the Bund): Vol. 1 *Kyōsanshugi* (Communism), Vol. 4 *Puroretaria tsūshin* (Proletarian Bulletin) (Hihyōsha).

scattered here and there, and finally found this book in a corner of the bookcase in my house in Kyoto. The price was 150 yen (50 cents in those days). When I riffled through it, the dust caused me to sneeze.

In January 1960, Takaaki (Ryūmei) Yoshimoto, the poet and philosopher, wrote an article titled "Political Thought of the Postwar Generation," published in *Chūō Kōron*, the monthly well-respected by the intelligentsia of the time.[3] In this article, Yoshimoto mentioned, along with authors like Shintarō Ishihara and Kenzaburō Ōe, whose names were already established, the writings of Reiji Himeoka, as an example of the thinking of "political activists of the young generation," that is, the student movement activists along the lines of the Bund. He noted that in contrast to Ishihara and Ōe who readily ignored (at least until that time) the prewar and wartime past as something they did not experience, the political activists of the young generation had developed their particular political ideology from the analysis of an overall vision of societal structure that carried through from the prewar to wartime to postwar periods. While acknowledging the weight that the imperial system placed on the prewar and postwar societal structure, he stated that, though there were differences in assessments due to differences in the experience of the war, as to the point that the revision of the Security Treaty was laying the groundwork for the maintenance and strengthening of state monopoly, he acknowledged an ideological commonality between the younger generation activists and himself.

This article by Yoshimoto came out just after the Zengakuren had caught the attention of the public with the November 1959 demonstration at the Diet, and it caused a sensation in the press. Some ten years later, in the special issue on Takaaki Yoshimoto, *Gendai Shi Techō* (Modern Poetry Notebook), it noted "this article was presented with such meaning as to separate the generations."[4] For us in the Bund, who had been fighting in isolation in both ideological and political spheres, this article meant the appearance of the golden opportunity of gaining a strong ally. This was indeed a message of solidarity sent to us, the "postwar generation who have formed themselves through individual will within the postwar monopolistic society," from a rare ideological thinker born of the "disillusioned generation" whose illusions were dashed and who were bound by "strictures of the state and ethnological constraints."

However, as I will note later, at the time of the collapse of the Bund, there were also harsh theoretical attacks that the "Himeoka state monopolistic capitalism theory" was responsible for the defeat of the anti-Security Treaty struggle. This may be the reason that the name "Himeoka," whether for good or ill, remains as a shared symbol in the collective memory of our generation that spent that political season together. Yet I, myself, had erased it from my consciousness while I was in the U.S. as there was no one around me who made an issue of it.

---

[3] Yoshimoto, Takaaki. "Sengo sedai no seiji shisō" (Political ideology of the postwar generation) in *Itan to seikei* (Heterodoxy and orthodoxy) (Gendai Shichōsha: 1960).

[4] Yoshimoto, Takaaki. *Gendai shi techō rinzō: Yoshimoto Takaaki* (Modern poetry notebook special supplement: Takaaki Yoshimoto) (Shichōsha: 1971).

If I may digress, I met Takaaki Yoshimoto, with whom I had such an important ideological encounter, just once. After the anti-Security Treaty struggle, as I was editing a journal, I visited his home with three comrades to request an article from him. We sat around a small table and Mr. Yoshimoto slowly poured green tea for us in four cups. Watching him, I felt the spirit of tea of the common people. When I pour tea for my family, I can still see Mr. Yoshimoto's manner in my mind's eye, and chastise myself for being so impatient.

Chapter 5
Nouvelle Vague

In reference to the "Nouvelle Vague" ("New Wave") of the late 1950s film makers in France, the leadership selected at the 14th Zengakuren convention in the spring of 1959 came to be called the New Wave of the student movement.[1] Until then members of the Communist Party, who were practically activists by occupation, had led the Zengakuren. In contrast, the new officers were from the new generation unencumbered by politics. Our average age was just over 21. This shift toward younger leadership was the brilliant idea of Shigeo Shima, the secretary general of the Bund.

But I thought I was miscast when he ordered me to remain on the executive committee of the Zengakuren as propaganda director. I felt more comfortable focusing on writing articles backstage rather than being onstage, and that I would be more useful that way. More than anything, I wanted to study. But when Shima's daring plan was applauded by everyone, I couldn't withdraw.

The centerpiece of Shima's plan was his persuasion of Kentarō Karōji, a student at the liberal arts faculty at Hokkaido University who was mostly unknown at the center, as his choice for Chair. Familiar with the works of Rimbaud, Camus, and Malraux, it was as if the term Nouvelle Vague was meant for Karōji. His speeches were inspiring, and with his handsome face he was popular with both men and women. At his post-election press conference, he shocked the reporters by asserting, "We'll engage in strikes and demonstrations with genuine spontaneity."

Within this unique group, our activism in the Zengakuren began in an enjoyable manner, contrary to what I had predicted. I went daily to the Zengakuren office

[1] I think it was Mainichi Shimbun social issues reporter Masahiro Yoshino, who often came to the Zengakuren office in those days, who first began using the term "nouvelle vague." He was about ten years older than I, but Karōji and I would go out drinking with him and we would talk about films. He was a fan of Jeanne Moreau, who starred in "Jules and Jim." Quite a few years later, at Katase Enoshima station on the Odakyū Line, he reprimanded the behavior of some hot-rodder gang members and was beaten to death by a metal chain. It pained me to learn of his death. This was the kind of fervent person he was.

M. Aoki, *Transboundary Game of Life*,
https://doi.org/10.1007/978-981-13-2757-5_5

at Kinsuke-cho, just beyond Motofuji Police Station near University of Tokyo's Yayoi gate, hardly ever going to the classrooms of the Economics Faculty where I was a student. This office was a shack with a couple of small rooms. Secretary Takeo Shimizu sat at the only desk, his face genial when he smiled with his missing teeth. The rest of the furniture consisted of a telephone that Shimizu used, several half-broken chairs, a pot-bellied stove, and a stand for the mimeograph machine, an indispensable technology in those pre-word processor days. It was like the club room of a university club.

For our meetings we took over the second floor of a nearby soba noodle shop. It was amazing that the shop owner didn't complain when we hung around for hours, only paying for one bowl of soba each. For our secret talks, we used a gallery cafe called Rouault in Hongō Sanchōme. It was a luxury for us to pay one hundred yen for curry always with a carefully portioned small piece of beef and potato and a demitasse of coffee.[2] The Zengakuren funds came from membership fees of the participating university self-governments and the fundraising that we did at Ochanomizu station. Our expenses were the often-late rent to the landlord next door and the rather considerable telephone charges. If one of us got some money, we would go out to Kabuki-chō in Shinjuku or nearby Okachimachi to drink cheap alcohol.

We also went to the orgs at universities around the country, from Hokkaido to Western Japan, to Kyushu. Thanks to these trips to major university campuses throughout Japan, I made all sorts of friends with whom I still keep in touch. It was too dangerous, though, for us to approach Nagoya University or Kobe University, whose self-governments were still under the control of the Communist Party. In August 1959, I went with Karōji and others to Hiroshima, jostled on a packed overnight train for twelve hours. This was to attend the annual general meeting of the Japan Council against Atomic and Hydrogen Bombs. There we made such pronouncements as "opposition to the Security Treaty is essential for opposing atomic and hydrogen bombs," and "we need to oppose nuclear bomb tests by the Soviet Union also." This shocked the activists in the Communist Party and General Council of Trade Unions who were attempting to make the opposition movement to nuclear weapons part of their vested interests under the guise of unifying a wide scope of the masses who were against nuclear weapons. It was a time when we had fun causing this type of disruption.

But this fun and idyllic time was about to end. On November 27 of that year, student and worker demonstrators protesting the revision of the U.S.-Japan Security Treaty broke through the front gates of the National Diet Building. The demonstrators withdrew of their own accord several hours later, but arrest warrants were issued for

[2]This coffee shop later closed. But from what I hear the employees bought the furniture and opened a shop with the same menu across from the front gate of the University of Tokyo. I dropped by when I was at Tōdai for a seminar recently. The nostalgic flavor of the curry rice was the same, but the price was 950 yen. Does this mean that the consumer price index has risen ten times in the last half-century? The layout of the store was much smaller than the long building with a courtyard in our day, and it no longer seemed to be a fitting space for plotting "revolutionary conspiracies."

Takeo Shimizu and Takeo Hayama of the Tokyo University Midori-kai (Faculty of Law student union), and they holed up on the University of Tokyo campus. Tensions rose as the small Zengakuren office filled with reporters. Two weeks later, as they led a demonstration, these two were arrested just outside the campus.

From my vantage point at the front of the demonstrators, I could tell that our storming of the National Diet Building was a spontaneous happening. As we were pressing against the guards, the front gate happened to open. The slogan "to the Diet!" of Socialist Party politicians unexpectedly came true. For about two hours inside the Diet Building, the students and workers who were demonstrating felt festive and excited at this amazing turn of events. Karōji had gone that day to Kyushu to organize, and he rushed back, but he was frustrated that he hadn't been there. Meanwhile, the mass media, which had been advocating for "democratic" and "anti-authoritarian" methods, denounced the demonstration as "the worst scandalous event in constitutional history."

The imposing structure of the Diet Building is most certainly the symbol of the authority of the parliamentary system. What occurred that day can be said to have raised the opportunity to rethink the meaning of what should be behind that symbol. This kind of event is not nor should become "routine." But as later developments proved, the authority of the parliament is not ultimately protected by its imposing structure; it cannot exist without the approval of its actions by its citizens, the masses. This event that raised a fundamental shared awareness was the harbinger of "the greatest test in constitutional history." In the short term, whether to storm the Diet again became the symbol dividing the position and determination of people in this season of anti-Security Treaty politics.

The Haneda Airport incident in the new year could no longer be considered spontaneous, but was quite intentional. As I noted earlier, over 70 demonstrators, including myself, were arrested.

My increasing involvement in these spontaneous and intentional events was due to being immersed in that era. But what kind of power was working within myself as an individual? To answer this query I will consider the temperament (should I say DNA?) that I inherited from my forebears.

Chapter 6
From Whence My DNA

In prewar days, it was apparently not unusual for a midwife to be the go between in introducing marriage prospects. No doubt this was because she was familiar with the families she served and had a good network of information. My parents were introduced to each other in this way and married. My father had graduated from the Faculty of Economics at University of Tokyo and worked at Mitsui Bussan trading company; and my mother was the eldest daughter of a small-scale businessman. The midwife thought that "this is a good match between a poor but educated man and a somewhat wealthy household," and most likely brought this prospect to my father's mother and my mother's father. (My father's father had already passed away.) My mother agreed, thinking that marrying someone who worked for a trading company may give her the chance to go abroad. But that hope soon evaporated with the outbreak of the Pacific War.

Apparently, my grandmother on my father's side was a descendant of the Murakami Suigun, the sea lords known as "the greatest pirate force of Japan" or "samurai who lorded over the great seas." She was born on Innoshima, a stronghold of the Murakami sea force that held sway over the Inland Sea during Japan's feudal period. Based on my vague memory of hearing this story from my father, I wrote about it in a newspaper series. Reading this, a local journalist looked into the history and obtained more detailed information.[1] My grandmother's father, my great grandfather, Tadaemon Aoki, was born into a family that owned a cargo ship. Perhaps because of his navigating abilities, he became captain of the Mikaho-maru, a warship of the Tokugawa Shogunate. Under Vice-Commander Takeaki Enomoto, who was displeased with the transfer of power back to the Emperor and planned to found the "Republic of Ezo," the Mikaho-maru, with seven consort ships, escaped off Shinagawa. A typhoon off Chōshi shipwrecked the vessel. This isn't a very heroic story, but if this failure hadn't happened, I would not have existed.

---

[1]Information according to reporter Tadashi Aoki of *Setouchi Taimusu* (Setouchi Times). I relied on material in *Innoshima shi shi* (Innoshima city history), pp. 825–827; Hirasawa, Fumihito, *Sengokubune Mukunoura* (Cargo ships in Mukunoura), pp. 237–239.

M. Aoki, *Transboundary Game of Life*,
https://doi.org/10.1007/978-981-13-2757-5_6

Having survived this ordeal, my great grandfather married a lady-in-waiting he met in Edo (now Tokyo) and returned to Innoshima where they had three daughters, my grandmother being the third one. They and the other daughters died soon after. My grandmother who was orphaned went to Tokyo, relying on her mother's family, and became a maid for the head clerk of a large business concern. Eventually she became the head maid, married my grandfather, an employee of one of the group companies, and bore six sons and one daughter. In an age when the rate of university graduates was still low, and despite the financial difficulties of losing her husband rather young, she was a realist who succeeded in sending all her sons to university. My father was her third son.

On the other side, my great grandfather on my mother's side was from the family of a low-level retainer in the former Tokugawa Shogunate. His older brother was slain in Kyoto for being a supporter of the Shogunate; and his younger brother died in battle in the Satsuma Rebellion (1877). My great grandfather survived and started a printing business after the Meiji Restoration. But, true to the adage, "a warrior's business sense," he lost his fortune. Going into debt, he purchased the latest large-size gas engine printing press from Germany, which blew up due to faulty operation twenty days after installation.

My grandfather Shūzo Nishihara was unable to fulfill his hopes to go to university. While working at a government office, he studied water control and waste water processing on his own to acquire specialized knowledge, and went to night school to learn English. During World War I he founded the Nishihara Hygienic Engineering Company and began a business in 1917. When that reached a sure footing, he went on his own to the U.S. and Europe to absorb advanced environmental technologies. He was then in his early 40s.

In postwar years, as his business grew steadily, my grandfather gained international recognition as a researcher. He was ever proud of the letter he received from Professor Gordon Fair of Harvard University, an authority on water treatment technology, citing him as "leaving a major contribution" to the field. As a youngster, I was awestruck at seeing my grandfather, sitting properly in his kimono every night after his work at the company, immersed in environmental technology development as he worked his slide rule.

If I say I inherited from my father's ancestors the DNA of the "seafarer's tendency" to go outward onto the seas and from my grandfather on my mother's side the DNA of the "entrepreneurial researcher spirit," it might be a good fit to explain my "trans-boundary life." But that DNA saw failure as well as success. There were luck and coincidence as well as the backing of the times. I had thought mine was a very ordinary family, but when I traced my family's background it seems there was quite a bit of drama. I feel more than ever that the Meiji Restoration was really a time of storm and stress that swept people up in a state of life changes. It might have been fate that both Prime Minister Nobusuke Kishi and Communist Party General Secretary Kenji Miyamoto were from Chōshū, the winning side, and my ancestors on both sides were on the Shogunate side, the losing side of the Meiji Restoration. The two sides of my family background are from Edo and the Inland Sea, whose cultures do not easily harmonize; and I saw this growing up as my parents had their differences.

Within me, as well, I feel conflicted at the appearance of opposing characteristics: the showiness of the Edoite versus the coarseness of the sea farer; idealism and optimism versus realistic calculation; favoring the new versus holding fast to the old. Yet it is this sort of uncertainty and contradiction that makes life and human beings interesting.

Turning to a different time and place, there is a named chair at Stanford University called the "Shuzo Nishihara Professorship in Environmental and Resource Economics" (Fig. 6.1). A named chair is a rank above regular tenured professorship at American universities, and a scholar who is a leading specialist in the field designated by the donor is appointed to that chair. At Stanford there are some 400 chaired professorships.[2] The Nishihara chair, named for Shūzō Nishihara, my grandfather, is the first environmental and resource economics chair at a major American university. My uncle, who succeeded my grandfather as president of the company, donated the funds for this chair in 1993 in recognition of my grandfather's achievements on the occasion of the hundredth anniversary of the founding of Stanford University.[3]

Stanford University spent several years seeking a scholar who could fill that chair, but it was not easy to find a suitable recipient as environmental economics was not well-established. Recruiting a young scholar with a bright future from Harvard University as an associate professor, they waited for his achievements to build, and named him to the chair some ten years later. Professor Lawrence Goulder is seen as one of the leading environmental economists, and since 2009 has jointly held the position of chair of the Economics Department. He has also drafted the carbon gas emission regulation law for California, said to be the strictest in the U.S. His office is right next to mine. I am sure my grandfather must be very happy with this outcome.

---

[2]The first endowed chair established at Stanford University was for some reason the Eiichi Shibusawa Chair; currently no professor occupies that chair.

[3]For contributions to industrial innovations made by Shūzō Nishihara, see Maeda (2008), pp. 69–73; 170–173.

The Shuzo Nishihara Professorship in Environmental and Resource Economics

Lawrence H. Goulder

Lawrence H. Goulder was appointed to this professorship in 2001. He is also a senior fellow of Stanford's Institute for International Studies, a research associate at the National Bureau of Economic Research, and a university fellow of Resources for the Future, a nonprofit environmental and natural resource research firm located in Washington, D.C.

Professor Goulder graduated from Harvard College with an A.B. in philosophy in 1973. He obtained a master's degree in musical composition from the Ecole Normale de Musique de Paris in 1975 and earned a Ph.D. in economics from Stanford in 1982. He was a faculty member in economics at Harvard before returning to Stanford's economics department in 1989.

Professor Goulder's research examines the environmental and economic impacts of U.S. and international environmental policies. He has focused considerably on policies to reduce emissions of "greenhouse gases" that contribute to climate change, and on "green tax reform"—revamping the tax system to introduce taxes on pollution and reduce taxes on labor effort or investment. To analyze environmental policies, Professor Goulder often employs a general equilibrium analytical framework that integrates the economy and the environment and links the activities of government, industry, and households. His work considers both the aggregate benefits and costs of various policies as well as the distribution of policy impacts across industries, income groups, and generations.

In collaborative work with biologists and climatologists, Professor Goulder has examined the philosophical and empirical bases for valuing ecosystem services, the connections between rates of population growth and levels of industrial pollution, and the potential to stimulate cost-reducing technological innovation through climate-change policies. He has conducted analyses for several government agencies and environmental organizations.

Professor Goulder was co-winner of the Erik Kempe Prize, awarded at the 1998 World Congress of Environmental and Resource Economists for the best environmental economics paper published within the last two years.

Shuzo Nishihara

This professorship was established in 1992 with gifts from the group of companies founded by Mr. Shuzo Nishihara and his family. The gifts were made in commemoration of the 75th anniversary of the founding of the first of the Nishihara companies, to honor Mr. Nishihara's foresight and accomplishments in the field of environmental sanitation, and in the hope of encouraging others to continue the search for solutions to environmental problems with the same enthusiasm that Mr. Nishihara sustained throughout his long and productive life.

Mr. Nishihara was born in Tokyo in 1883. He spent his youth helping with his father's business in the difficult early years of Japan's modernization and had few opportunities to gain a formal education. Although primarily self-taught, he had great ambitions and decided early in life that he would devote himself to promoting social justice and improving the quality of life through work in environmental sanitation, a field then virtually unknown to the Japanese public. He quit his job as a technician with the local government and, at the age of 34, established the Nishihara Engineering Co., Ltd., a firm specializing in the design, installation, and operation of sewage treatment facilities and related water supply and drainage equipment. The company rapidly expanded into one of Japan's leading sanitation engineering firms, a position it still holds. In 1957 wastewater treatment operations were transferred to an independent subsidiary, the Nishihara Environmental Sanitation Research Co., Ltd., which immediately assumed a key role in the nation's water pollution prevention program.

Success in business did not make Mr. Nishihara any less a scientist and engineer. If anything, he worked harder at sewage treatment technology research than at his administrative duties. The NEO High-Rate Digestion Process he developed was a creative breakthrough that won patents in Japan and abroad. He received the Medal of Yellow Ribbon in 1955 and the Order of the Sacred Treasure, Gold Rays with Rosette in 1965 from the Japanese government.

Mr. Nishihara and his wife Masu, whom he married in 1909, had 1 son and 4 daughters, and were blessed with 12 grandchildren. He died in 1965 at the age of 82.

37

Fig. 6.1 Shūzō Nishihara (right) and Prof. Goulder (left) in Stanford University article

Chapter 7
Childhood

I was born on April 1, 1938, April Fool's Day, in Nagoya, where my father was posted at the trading company where he was employed. About a year later we moved to Mita, in Tokyo, where my father had grown up. From the time I can remember we lived in the Shōnan coast area, in Kugenuma and Katase (Fig. 7.1). My father was drafted into the military when I was very young. As a university graduate employed by a trading company, he would have been given a post like accounting, but for some reason he applied to be a regular soldier and was sent to China. At times he wrote letters to families of soldiers who didn't know how to write. Having been bullied by his unit commander, who had only a grade school education, he was occasionally beset by nightmares even after the end of the war. He said that years later he happened to bump into this former commander, who dashed away from him. After that he no longer had those bad dreams.

Fig. 7.1 At Shōnan Beach, about two or three years old

M. Aoki, *Transboundary Game of Life*,
https://doi.org/10.1007/978-981-13-2757-5_7

My first clear childhood memory is of the night the Pacific War began when I was three and a half years old. For some reason my mother, younger sister, and I were staying in the second story of a house out in the country on the Izu Peninsula. We were scolded by a local person who was making the security rounds of the neighborhood that the light from the room was shining out the window, and we quaked in fear.

Until we received a notice from the city office in mid-March 1944 that those born on April 1 were to start school that year, my parents didn't know this, and we were surprised that I was suddenly to enter grade school. I was an introvert, and when my mother went away to fill out some forms during the entrance ceremony, I became upset and wailed loudly. But when I began to go to school, my extrovert nature came out, and my high-pitched voice could be heard, "kin, kin" on the way home, so I was called "Kin-chan" by our neighbors. Years later, when I was about to depart for the U.S. and went to say my goodbyes to the mother of a famed woman critic who lived nearby, she told me, "Please go quietly." The impression I left as Kin-chan must have been very strong. In grade school I was good at drawing pictures, and was asked if my father was an artist.

When the air raids started, my grandfather rented a house in Sengataki, Karuizawa, in Nagano Prefecture, so that the women (my mother and aunts) and children could evacuate to the countryside. I was happy that I could live almost like siblings with my uncle who was only five years older than I. The pseudo-militaristic comics that he shared with me—"Norakuro," "Hatchan the Octopus," "Adventurous Dankichi"—gave me, a child, a glimpse into the wider world, in an age when there was no television. I was what they called an "evacuee kid," but I don't recall having been bullied. When I teased a local boy classmate that his red celluloid sheet to slide under his notebook page was "like a girl's," he told me, "It's all right because we're in a critical time." This made sense to me as I understood what the war meant to us.

After the entire family gathered to hear the Emperor's radio broadcast ending the war, my grandmother brought out some lumps of sugar that she had put away somewhere and, as she gave them to us children, told us, "Now is the time when you children have to do your best." When we returned to our home in Katase, I went to the beach and saw a fleet of black American battleships moored in Sagami harbor. To my child's mind, it was as if the black ships had come again, the harbinger of a new age. Tanks came up on land at nearby Tsujidō beach.

With the dissolution of the *zaibatsu* group companies my father lost his job and began to work at the company run by my grandfather on my mother's side. My father became a loyal head clerk company man, working for my entrepreneurial grandfather, and my relationship with him became rather indifferent. It was only in my father's latter years that I felt we came to understand each other.

When I returned from evacuating to the countryside, I entered Shōnan Gakuen, a private school. The PTA chair was a businessman who had been educated in Britain in prewar times. He recruited Masami Miyashita from the kindergarten of Keio Gijuku to be the head of school, which espoused liberal education under the motto "bring sunshine into our hearts." The school building was in a pine grove, and our playground was sandy. During class time we put out fertilizer and grew sweet potatoes. They were what are called organic vegetables these days. During and after the war when there were food shortages, our main nutrition was from vegetables grown in the garden, and we ate a lot of sweet potatoes and squash. It is only recently that I have come to think dishes of dried daikon radish and pumpkin soup taste good.

Every morning I left my house at seven o'clock and walked thirty minutes through a pine grove to go to school. This was to play three-bases before classes started. Years later the late Gaitei Kanakubo, who became the head of the golf team at Keio University, told me, "You were really crazy about sports but lousy at it." Most of my classmates were Yomiuri Giants baseball fans, but being a contrarian, I was a diehard Hanshin Tigers fan. It was the time of the explosive "dynamite battery" of Tomio Fujimura and Kaoru Betto and Wakabayashi was throwing his "seven-colored unhittable pitches." Our distant relative was the head umpire for professional baseball, and perhaps because of that, my uncle, who was a baseball fan, took me at times to Kōrakuen Stadium. In Akira Kurosawa's "Stray Dog" there is a scene showing the tension of a full baseball stadium with everyone's feelings as one. That scene brilliantly captures the vigor of the spirit of that time when the country was rising from the wartime wasteland.

Unlike my memories of playing, I have hardly any memories of studying. During summer vacation I spent every day rapt in swimming and fishing, and never wrote in my diary. My summer homework notebook had many blank pages. My mother scolded me severely for this. Social studies was the exception, and I read the "Boys Asahi Yearbook" which my parents bought for me from cover to cover. It was full of domestic and international news and information about nature, which might be like compulsively reading Wikipedia these days. I must have had a nerdy streak in that area.

I also created a class newspaper. One morning before class we were told that our teacher Mr. Eda, who had kindly watched such efforts from eyes deep behind his glasses, would no longer be coming to school. From the talk of grownups I learned that he was dismissed because of something called the "red purge." This happened in 1949.

Chapter 8
Middle School Years

At Shōnan Gakuen, the entrepreneurial head of school Ms. Miyashita had founded the middle school after the grade school, and in 1950 my class became the third to enter middle school there. The classroom building was next to a rice paddy, a school building no longer in use that had been minimally restored. There was an area we called the "haunted house" which was dangerous and off limits. Contrary to its outward appearance, in reality the school offered a meaningful experience. The family backgrounds of the students were diverse, ranging from former major industrialists, former lords, leaders in the economic world to ordinary company employees, shopkeepers, single parents; and the students' abilities were all over the map in terms of talents, strengths, academics, IQ, and athletics. It was a positive time for postwar democracy that overcame the status consciousness of the old order, and boys and girls played together in a friendly manner. Recently I attended a class reunion which brought back vivid memories of classmates from decades ago.

Seated next to me in my second year was Masaaki Hirao. Before classes began, he would use the teacher's dais as a stage and make the classroom roll with laughter at his comic narratives. He was full of volunteering spirit from middle school days and went to nursing homes to perform comic narratives and helped me, tone-deaf, by singing with me to pass the music test.

One time, Hirao and I got into an argument in the classroom, and ended up slapping each other. The class started, so I controlled myself with difficulty, but he landed another punch. The girl sitting behind me cried out, "That's horrible!" This all happened so quickly the teacher didn't notice. After the class, Hirao bought a bottle of milk at lunchtime and handed it to me without a word. It was seven years later when I was immersed in the student movement that he created such a sensation with his "rockabilly storm" teaming up with Mickey Curtis and Keijirō Yamashita that girls would faint at their performances. They were called "music biker groups," which has something in common with what I was called as we were both pounded by the waves of the times (Fig. 8.1).

One person with whom I got along well for some reason and still have a close friendship is Ken'ichi Sekiya. He continued his father's company's cutting technique

M. Aoki, *Transboundary Game of Life*,
https://doi.org/10.1007/978-981-13-2757-5_8

Fig. 8.1 On stage in school play with Masaaki Hirao (left)

using whetstones, and developed it into a precision slicing technique that can slice a single strand of hair into ten segments. His company became Disco Corporation with a significant market share of the world's semiconductor fabrication equipment. He seemed to be good at grasping the crux of techniques, and even in middle school excelled in many areas like karate, long distance swimming, and abalone hunting. He became chair of the World Semiconductor Council and has a home in Silicon Valley, so he has become a part time neighbor of mine.

There were others among the galaxy of notables in my class. One person who gave me intellectual stimulation was Yūji Takahashi, who was in the class a year below mine, and a fellow member of the Literary Arts Club—a club with just three members. He later became internationally renowned as a progressive composer and pianist. He was clearly a prodigy from his middle school years, and even our teachers were in awe of him. He would walk into upper level classes as he pleased, and delved into Latin and Greek textbooks on his own.

In 1967, when I was in Boston, he woke me up with an early morning phone call. I thought he might be arranging to go eat some oysters in the morning, but he said, "Something's strange, I've lost my memory." I rushed to him, wondering if his genius brain had reached its limit, to find that he had forgotten that he was married and that he had come to play with the Boston Symphony Orchestra. A little while later I found out that he had slipped on the ice and had hit his head.

During middle school I learned from him about all sorts of progressive ideas. Joyce, Kafka, surrealism, Dadaism, dodecaphonic music, and it goes without saying, Marx. After school we would wander into used bookstores in Kamakura to get books to read. This was the time that the seeds were sown for my later participation in the student movement.

My mother, fearing for my future as I was attracted to these maverick ideas and not interested in my studies, asked her friend who was a typist at the American Embassy to tutor me in English. Some six months later, my grades had gone up, and they went from being just above middling to become the top in my third year of middle school.

As I bid farewell to my enjoyable middle school life, I was hit with a bolt out of the blue.

Chapter 9
High School Years

In those days, entering high school from Shōnan Gakuen meant that the wealthy students went to Keiō Gijuku High School, and the students from middle class income families with decent grades chose the prefectural public Shōnan High School. I had no doubt that I could get into Shōnan High School. This was because the selection could be done with just a transcript from middle school.

But I was beset with an unforeseen happening. I suffered from severe stomach pain from a few months before April 1953 when I was to enter high school. A medical doctor at University of Tokyo, who was to treat the leukemia suffered by fishermen who were irradiated from the hydrogen bomb test at Bikini atoll the next year, often dropped by our house on Sundays during his walks. He took a look at me and pronounced, "It's probably just worms," so we left it alone. That was a mistake. In the end the pain was so great I couldn't even stay lying down, and when I stood up, I fainted. My appendix had burst and I was in a critical state from the infection throughout my abdominal area. Fortunately, my life was saved by a capable surgeon, and I was given streptomycin, which was a new antibiotic at the time. Later my mother told me the sad story of a case she saw when she was in the hospital when she was young and such medicine wasn't available. A child who was admitted to the hospital in just the same state as I asked to eat the thin paper surrounding castella cake as he died.

I was in the hospital for a few weeks. My classmates came by to see me, making me laugh, which hurt my stomach. I was happy that the girls in my class also came by. But when I was released from the hospital and went to look at the names of students who had been accepted to the high school, my name wasn't there. While the doctor had written "peritonitis" on the medical report, the person in charge at Shōnan High School had noted "tuberculous peritonitis." My teacher at Shōnan Gakuen Middle School spoke up for me, but the decision could not be overturned.

This was the first major setback in my life and I was dejected. But I am rather strong when I am beaten down, so I felt that what had occurred couldn't be helped. My parents bought me a record player to cheer me up. When I listened to Tchaikovsky's

M. Aoki, *Transboundary Game of Life*,
https://doi.org/10.1007/978-981-13-2757-5_9

Fig. 9.1 Author (second right) with classmates from Koyamadai High School

"Pathetique," it seemed to me that my parents were the ones who were in a sad state of mind.

Fortunately, Shōnan Gakuen had started a high school, so I took emergency refuge there. I continued my habit of going around used bookstores in Kamakura with Yūji Takahashi, but with university entrance exams looming ahead, I couldn't keep doing that. I took a test for transfers to enter Koyamadai High School in Tokyo, where my cousin a few years older than I had been close to since our days in Karuizawa during the war attended, and entered there. That year, seventy students had not been allowed to move up to the second year of High School, and they all went to other schools, so there were openings for transfers. At that time, it was one of the top ten high schools for students who entered University of Tokyo. Yūji Takahashi went to Tōhō Girls' High School Music Department (which was co-ed), that had just been founded with the participation of his teacher, the composer Minao Shibata (Fig. 9.1).

When I started at Koyamadai, unlike at Shōnan Gakuen, there was only one other student who wore his hair long. The others all had buzz cuts. By the time we graduated, nearly everyone had long hair. In contrast to the elite Hibiya High School, Koyamadai High School, located in the midst of the commercial district along the Mekama rail line, still retained the simple Spartan quality and sense of the commoner of the prewar era schools. Among the teachers who had taught there from the prewar system, there were real professionals who taught mathematics and English. The mathematics education I received there was good preparation for the first year graduate course in real number solutions in the U.S.

One teacher I remember well was my homeroom teacher Masatatsu Maita who taught Chinese classics. He was only about forty years old, but with his mustache and elusive quality, he seemed to be an aged sage who had emerged from the Chinese classics. Some twenty years later I became deeply engaged with China, and this encounter with the teacher nicknamed Okera, Penniless, may have foreshadowed my future. Mr. Maita pretended not to see when we drank and were rowdy, but he was stern when he had to be. I attended the memorial party for Mr. Maita when he passed away, at age 90, in 2006. Former Deputy Minister of International Trade Makoto Kuroda and Vice Minister Nobutsugu Fukugawa were at Koyamadai High School as well. It seems Hibiya High School graduates went into the Finance Ministry while Koyamadai High School graduates went into the Ministry of International Trade and Industry. This might have had something to do with the differing characters of the schools.

Hiroshi Arai, a classmate who sat right behind me, was kind to me, a transfer student, and he showed me ways to think about science and math problems, which I wasn't good at. After graduating from Tokyo Institute of Technology, he became an engineer, and taking early retirement issued a book on points in dispute in archaeology from the scientific perspective, upsetting some of the preconceptions in archaeology. He also taught at a Korean university. Next to me sat Yūzō Nakanishi, who wasn't into studying but was a baseball slugger. During practice in the small schoolyard, he would hit fly balls which smashed into classroom windows. This was why the windows on the second and third stories of the school were fitted with metal screens. Thanks to his batting ability, our high school reached the top sixteen among Tokyo high schools. When he went to university and saw how the famous baseball player Shigeo Nagashima practiced, he realized he was no match and gave up baseball. Now he runs a recycle business, which is economically practical. He is one who looks after people well, and he helped me when I was involved in the relocation to Canada of a Chinese economist who defected just after the Tiananmen Square incident. I still meet up for drinks with these high school friends from the good old days, who are a bit different from my friends at Shōnan Gakuen.

My studies for the university entrance exam progressed smoothly, and as Arai and I tested ourselves taking mock exams for Surugadai cram school and University of Tokyo guidance meetings, I went as far as placing tenth in the nation. That was when I had a vague idea of becoming a historian. I went to the used book store area of Jinbōchō and collected books written by Marxist historians such as Tadashi Ishimoda and Moriaki Araki.

I was able to enter University of Tokyo without incident. But there, as I wrote before, I met up with unforeseen events which changed my life.

Chapter 10
Sugamo Prison and Anti-security Treaty Struggle

For two weeks after I was arrested at Haneda Airport in January 1960, I was detained at the police station at Akihabara, Tokyo. As I had maintained my silence, the attending prosecutor, perhaps to teach me a lesson, sent me to Sugamo Prison. This was where Richard Sorge of the Sorge espionage incident and Hideki Tōjō and other A-level war criminals were imprisoned and executed. Nobusuke Kishi had also been detained there as a war criminal. Now it was my turn, as I had opposed his politics. Now a skyscraper called Sunshine City has been built on that spot.

My life in prison was rather comfortable. In a turnaround from the tumult of the combatant student movement, the small, clean solitary cell was isolated from the outside world. The only time I had contact with others was when the warden played catch ball with me in the prison courtyard. I took baths by myself, and being forbidden newspapers and radio, the only thing I could do was to read books.

My lawyer brought me various books. I reread the economics works of Kōzō Uno and other books I had wanted to read but hadn't had a chance to. Uno economics was the original systemization of Marx's "Das Kapital" put forward by Professor Kōzō Uno of University of Tokyo, and its logic was popular among the Bund activists. I almost felt regret at bidding my farewell to the month of solitary confinement that I spent immersed in reading books.

Were my parents worried? I had no way of knowing because I was in prison, and I didn't want to know. But no doubt they were alarmed. I learned later that my room at Yayoi-chō in Hongō had been searched by the police for "violation of laws related to punishment of physical violence" who confiscated a leaflet; and that the Ministry of Education had issued a vice ministerial notification to each university president with the "demand to expel from the campus the malicious student leaders of the Zengakuren." But when I came out of prison, my parents seemed rather calm. This was because my grandfather, a liberal-thinking businessman, had checked my mother's agitation by saying, "It's a good thing that the young act to correct the politics of the old." My father worried that I might be expelled, and met with the chief administrator of the Economics Faculty, a high school friend of his, and was guaranteed that there was no issue; but seeing my grades, he was glum.

M. Aoki, *Transboundary Game of Life*,
https://doi.org/10.1007/978-981-13-2757-5_10

Waiting until all twenty-one Zengakuren and Bund leaders were released, the Bund general secretary Shigeo Shima gave his famous speech exhorting us to join the final complete opposition struggle aimed at the abrogation of the U.S.-Japan Security Treaty. His famous line was, "Either the Security Treaty falls apart or the Bund falls apart." Perhaps because I had been confined in prison, this speech did not resonate with me. I think there was also a difference in our temperaments. I was excited by spontaneous acts like the storming of the Diet the previous November, but I felt that organizing a struggle went beyond my abilities and my nature. I was well aware that I was not like Zengakuren chair Kentarō Karōji, who was able to express his commitment with resolute action.

The student movement of that time was based on class debates, with decisions about abandoning classes and holding strikes to be made at meetings of representatives selected in those debates. This followed the perfect model of postwar democracy. By that time the Bund and the Communist Party were in vigorous competition over the leadership of the self-government of the universities, but this was also based on mass debates. Many of the Communist Party affiliated student leaders, whom we in the Bund derisively called "Yoyogi" (the place name of the headquarters of the Japanese Communist Party), ended up leaving the Communist Party. But in those days, influenced by the Italian Communist Party's "structural reform line," they confronted us with soft and sophisticated arguments. Through such arguments the anti-Security Treaty student movement pulled workers and the general public into mass demonstrations that swelled to an unprecedented scale. I think no one, including Shima himself, could have imagined this would happen.

I am confident that I made as much effort as anyone to mobilize ordinary students to demonstrate at the Diet Building through discussions with them. We were also the group that was regarded with the greatest hostility by the Revolutionary Communist League (Kakukyōdō), an organization that concentrated on recruiting philosophical young people by claiming the need for establishment of a proletarian body to achieve a revolution while usurping the mass movement that the Bund had organized, as we clashed with them through discussions. But I did not participate in the planning of the "military" tactic of re-occupying the Diet Building. This was because I wasn't sure how a mass movement could evolve so quickly without losing the characteristics of a mass movement. On this point I was "sitting on the fence," as they say, but Shima and Kōji Ikuta left me alone on this. As I couldn't fall into place psychologically, the days passed as I continued to feel glum. I even thought my feelings would clear up if I could just join in the demonstrations as an ordinary student. I wasn't at the head of the June 15 demonstration which became bloody with the mobilization of the riot police and saw the death of Michiko Kanba, a Bund activist. As the events of that day had the characteristics of being a mass movement, my wavering was lacking in foresight, decisiveness, and courage.

Prime Minister Kishi considered ultimately mobilizing the Self Defense Forces, though denied this by the head of the Defense Agency. The Bund had no reserve of energy to organize more drastic movements; and on June 19 the Security Treaty revision was automatically approved by the Diet. With this, Prime Minister Kishi resigned, and the mass movement receded like the tide. Seeing this as the "defeat" of the Bund is the Bund's "orthodox history." I'm not making excuses, but I think there could be another way of looking at the situation. We could say that the anti-Security Treaty struggle meant the change of an era in that it changed the game of what the form of the country would be.

On one hand, there would be no future in the Kishi style of political options that called for the mobilization of military forces of the state to supplement the lack of their own ability for democratic governance. I understand that among those heads of businesses who led the economic growth in the ensuing years not a few considered that the anti-Security Treaty struggles removed the weight of the possibility of the revival of a controlled economy.[1] On the other hand, the "progressive party" myth that it would control and manage the spontaneous political actions of the masses and the illusion (actually only rhetoric?) that the working class would rise up to change the shape of the nation through violence were dashed. After this time, the government used the fruits of high rates of economic growth to take in the demands of various interest groups and aimed to instill political stability by awarding pluralistic interests; and the leftist political parties also had a share in playing a role in this type of mechanism.[2]

In any event, the Bund, by playing the most radical role in the fierce series of "incidents," unconsciously accomplished the role of catalyst leading to the next era. That is the very reason it was time for it to withdraw from history's stage. Before the curtain was drawn, there was another internal turmoil that it had to undergo.

---

[1]One such example is the following comment made by former Nomura Securities Chairman Setsuya Tabuchi in his "My Memoir." "I read Mr. Masahiko Aoki's memoir with interest. I am someone who is the opposite of those following communism, but I agreed with him in viewing the 1960 'Japan-U.S. Security Treaty' as a symbolic incident. Prime Minister Nobusuke Kishi was attempting to rule postwar Japan using the means of state capitalism that ruled former Manchukuo" (*Nihon Keizai Shimbun*, November 1, 2007).

[2]Although I was not in Japan at the time, the Zenkyōtō movement a decade later broke free from progressive mythology and revolutionary illusion to raise protests against the state of universities considered the norm up until that time. In that regard, it may be said to have been an even more fundamentally radical reform movement.

Chapter 11
Dissolution of the Bund

With the resignation of Prime Minister Kishi, the "season of politics" ended, and the Japanese were starting to face toward the "season of economics" with their energy poured into high rates of growth. The activists of the Bund had lost their goal and their way of thinking was in disarray.

In July 1960, about fifty representatives gathered from around the country to hold a Bund general meeting. When general secretary Shigeo Shima began his report in a sloppy way, in a complete turnaround from his famous speech in April, he was heckled and angry shouts were aimed at him. He had an asthma attack and couldn't continue. So Kōji Ikuta read his report in his place. When the discussion started, as I had psychologically and in actuality stepped down from tactical leadership, I had no counter argument as to who was responsible for why we couldn't continue the "revolutionary" struggle and why it had come to a "defeat," and could only keep silent.

As the discussion became ever more convoluted, we were informed that "the police have surrounded us and will step in at dawn," and the meeting was quickly adjourned. I wonder if this was a plot thought up by Ikuta and others to avoid further disarray, which would have surfaced if we had continued the meeting.

As those of us in the leadership—Shima, Satoshi Kitakōji who represented the chair of Zengakuren, Ikuta, and others—sat in a circle afterward, Shima muttered, "I thought I had created the Bund, but it was you." Taken aback, I couldn't understand what he meant. But it seemed he was shifting the blame onto me, and I was so chagrined that my eyes flooded with tears in front of all the others. It was only after I later read his writings that I was finally able to surmise what he meant by those words.

When I now dredge up the meaning of the "struggle" of that time, it seems to me that it was a microcosmic projection of various aspects of the thought structure of the Japanese.

The main character behind the scenes at that meeting was Kentarō Karōji who was still in prison. On April 26, at the start of the new school year, he clambered onto the riot police's armored truck blocking the boulevard leading to the front gate of the Diet

M. Aoki, *Transboundary Game of Life*,
https://doi.org/10.1007/978-981-13-2757-5_11

Fig. 11.1 Kentarō Karōji (in dark blazer) just before jumping over the armored truck; at left in student uniform is Kōichirō Shinohara, Student Socialist League Chair (*photo* Kōichirō Kasagawa)

Building grounds. He gave a fierce speech encouraging agitation, then barehanded, he jumped into the wave of riot police. Thousands of students and workers surged behind him. His existential act of literally throwing himself into the fray to express his commitment aroused the demonstrators' sympathies. The cameraman Kōichirō Kasagawa, who watched Karōji before he gave his speech through the cold eye of his camera lens recalls it this way: "Karōji's expression, which reminded me of a dour progressive poet, was memorable. All the time I watched him, he didn't say a word, neither did he change his expression. He just kept staring straight ahead" (Fig. 11.1).[1]

Shocked by this incident, the Bund affiliated with University of Tokyo made an about turn from its previous stance of mistrusting radical action.[2] In typical University of Tokyo student fashion, we did not neglect arming ourselves with theoretical backing. They claimed that my "Himeoka state monopolistic capitalist theory" did not discern the weakness of Japanese capitalism, which was scarcely being supported

[1] Kasagawa, Kōichirō, private correspondence (December 2007).

[2] In his record of the times, Shima criticizes the Tōdai faction as sitting on the fence during the midst of the anti-Security Treaty struggles, and then suddenly mounting a leftist attack at the Bund general meeting. (*Bunto shishi* (Personal history of the Bund), Hihyōsha). But I think this is a misconception on Shima's part.

by the government's monetary-fiscal policy, and thus lost a golden opportunity to overthrow it.[3]

When I later read what Shima, who was a student at University of Tokyo's Faculty of Medicine, wrote, "The reason the Bund fell apart was because I didn't know economic theory. That is why I began to study economics," I was able to surmise the true meaning of what he had previously muttered. But I suspect that for Shima, who spent his life carrying through his aspiration to right society's wrongs through his medical work in Okinawa, studying economics was a waste of time. The belief in the "supremacism of economics" in which rationalization for strategies of political action can be derived only from "economics," and the way of thinking that lacked a vision for overall social structure by insisting that state monopoly is maintained only by government policies may seem at first glance a way to rationalize extreme radicalism. But the frailty of this approach was unmasked when the temporary excitement cooled off. It was hardly surprising that the University of Tokyo faction of the Bund soon dispersed like mist.

One other behind the scenes main character was Kan'ichi Kuroda, the "blind philosopher" who cynically criticized from the edge the loose organizational structure of the Bund. I took part of my pen name from Lenin, but the organization of the Bund was a far cry from the Leninist principles of strict selection of organization participation (joining the party) and centralized administration to instill control of the organization. We recruited anyone who had the enthusiasm and ability to join the movement and anyone we thought would be useful to the movement. And the internal organizational structure was not authoritarian, but had the flexibility for ad hoc changes in influence and decision making authority depending on our discussions. When the tide of the movement ebbs, this kind of organization falls apart into anarchy at national meetings. Even without agreeing with Kan'ichi Kuroda's scheme-like methods, the idea that it was important to make steady efforts to organize in building a progressive party gained prominence within the Bund.

But I couldn't adapt myself at all to the sense of making the building of an organization my own goal. The way of thinking that sees the value of commonly sharing a fate brings about tragic results for individuals, as proven by later events. My greatest passion was to destroy the progressive myth of the old leftists that was supported only by words, and I gradually leaned toward thinking, "When that role is finished, it can't be helped if the Bund is dissolved."

This is the way my "first venture" dissolved within myself. But the idea that venture organizations should intermediate the individual's spontaneity and autonomy runs consistently through my incorrigible efforts at repeated attempts to launch ventures.

[3]The Tōdai faction critique of the Himeoka theory targeted item (3) in Footnote 10 of "Chap. 4: Reiji Himeoka."

Chapter 12
Fleeing the Frontline

In summer 1960, the song popular among former student activists was Sachiko Nishida's "After the Acacia Rain," with the line "pelted by the acacia rain, I just want to die."[1] My own feelings were to the contrary. I felt that I had finally reached rock bottom from which I could rise up.

The Bund members each had our own reasons for political realignments, and for all intents and purposes the organization disintegrated without a formal decision to disband or any clashes that risked everything. This was a positive feature of the Bund, as it was an autonomous and spontaneous agency of intermediation.

In actuality, though, a group of us, including the Zengakuren's Takeo Shimizu and Satoshi Kitakōjo who had just been released from prison, and Susumu Nishibe of University of Tokyo Komaba campus, attended to the disposition of matters. We publicly announced the reissuing of "Proletariat Bulletin," the organ of the Bund at its founding, and were called the "Pro Tsū ha" (Prol Bulletin faction), but as Marx said, "the second time is a farce." Besides our mutually shared negative impression of the demands made by the childish radicalism of the ultra-leftist Tōdai Faction (Revolutionary Communication Faction; Kakumei Tsūtatsu ha) and the Battle Flag Faction (Senki ha)'s establishment of a progressive party and its ideology of proletarian supremacy, we were just dragging along with our personal relationships formed at the Zengakuren office without engaging in any actual action. The Battle Flag Faction eventually made a thorough "philosophical" self-criticism that they lacked "self-awareness of radical identity" and went under the umbrella of the Kakukyōdō, let by "the blind philosopher" Kan'ichi Kuroda.

As we were wallowing in this state, all of the "Proletariat Bulletin faction" gathered in my small boarding room in Minami Aoyama, Tokyo, in March 1961. Shimizu and

[1]The Wikipedia article on this song notes that the dry vocals and decadent lyrics were associated with the young people who had become worn out by the anti-Security Treaty struggles. It also came to symbolize the defeat of the protest movement and was used as the background music in televised programs about the times, particularly the death of student Michiko Kanba and further protest demonstrations (Accessed January, 2008).

M. Aoki, *Transboundary Game of Life*,
https://doi.org/10.1007/978-981-13-2757-5_12

Kitakōji suggested we join with the Revolutionary Communist League (Kakukyōdō). Apparently, they thought the rest of us would all immediately follow their lead. But instantly, Nishibe said, "No way." I agreed with him without a second thought as I thought it was out of the question to bow down for political expediency and opportunism to those with incompatible ideology whom we had fought. The rest of the group felt the same way.

In his usual way, Shimizu blustered, "Are you guys going to flee the frontline?!" to which we flatly stated, "Yes, we're going to flee the frontline," as we were no longer old guard leftists. There were one or two others who said they would start a different progressive party on their own. Shimizu and Kitakōji looked to have pulled back for a second. When I brought out my broom and started sweeping my small room, they left, even though they looked like they were feeling regretful. That was the last of my interactions with them.

They later became party to the horrific violent infighting within the Revolutionary Communist League (Kakukyōdō). This was regrettable as they had gifts of rare talents. What made them undergo a "conversion" to Kakukyōdō? Just before this March meeting, Karōji was released from his long imprisonment and announced that he would go to the Kakukyōdō, taking with him the Battle Flag Faction, in typical Karōji style. This was a totally unexpected direction for us. Shocked by this, I think others rushed aboard so as not to be left behind. On Karōji's part there must have been anger about the chaos within the Bund that had arisen while he was gone, after he had put his all on the line to incite the struggle against the Security Treaty. Soon Karōji realized his "greatest mistake in life" and jumped ship from the Kakukyōdō. And he went manfully into prison in Utsunomiya.

In November 1963, when he completed his sentence and was released from prison, I went with Kōichirō Shinohara, chair of the Shagakudō (Student Socialist League), who had been released two months earlier, and Yoshinobu Tōhara, a Waseda University graduate with whom I had often gone drinking in the Zengakuren, to meet Karōji as he left prison. We weren't in a circumstance to hold a lively party to celebrate his release, nor could we think of anything in particular to do. We felt abashed and awkward. We ended up going to nearby Nikko to sightsee and drank beer at a tourist restaurant. We watched in silence the news of the Kennedy assassination being shown on television. After that, Karōji no longer involved himself in political activism. He had the courage to attempt to reset his life course when necessary. I wonder if, in the case of Shimizu and Kitakōji, they were unable to think of the option to escape from the political world once they had stepped into it.

As for me, although I had broken rank with political movements by "fleeing the frontline," I had not yet graduated from university. In February 1961 I had taken the exam to enter University of Tokyo's Graduate School of Applied Economics. Only two of us passed the written exam, but I was dropped after the second stage oral exam. This was without any meaningful question and answer session. The fact that I, a mere student, had published a book interpreting the Uno economic theory in my own way may have offended the professors who held up the validity of Uno studies faction.

Fig. 12.1 With my younger sister (two or three years after the anti-Security Treaty struggles)

This was the second academic exam failure for me, after my high school entrance exam. I had already added a year to my undergraduate career due to being imprisoned, and now I was to add another year. However, one can never tell what life holds, as this failure prevented me from being entrapped in Marxist academics, a direction that had no future.

During my extra year I translated the seminal work *The Permanent Revolution* in Trotsky's collected works which were being published then. And I read original works authored by leading modern economists published in the 1940s and 1950s that I purchased. They included Samuelson's *Foundations of Economic Analysis*, Debreu's *Theory of Value*, and Arrow's *Social Choice and Individual Values*. I no longer felt creative stimulation from academic Marxist economics that I had felt about Uno economic theory of my early days. My intellectual curiosity was piqued to learn about things I had not known.

The Haneda Airport incident trial began around that time. With twenty-one defendants in all, I left the hearings up to the other defendants and lawyers. When I ultimately received the sentence of four months' imprisonment with three years' probation, I felt quite unconnected from it.

One year later I took the exam for theoretical economics and was able to enter the graduate school at University of Tokyo. I was relieved that the conditions were finally set for me to concentrate on my studies. But this didn't mean the path of my intellectual course was fixed (Fig. 12.1).

Chapter 13
Toward Modern Economics

Upon entering graduate school, I joined a seminar taught by Yoshirō Tamanoi, an Uno economics follower who was a specialist on economic doctrinal history. Marxism was in its glory days in the Faculty of Economics at University of Tokyo, and there were not yet any seminars that seriously dealt with theories of modern economics. Professor Ryūtarō Komiya had just returned from studying abroad at Harvard University. To me, in the midst of the process of converting from Marxism, his razor-sharp features exuded an atmosphere that was difficult for me to approach.

In contrast the Tamanoi seminar, though originally one of Uno school Marxist economics, was influenced by Shunpei Kumon, later Director of the Global Communication Center at International University ((Fig. 13.1): front row third from right), and others, and was in the process of falling away from believing in Marx. So it was in a state of anything goes. The photograph was taken at a party for the seminar at Professor Tamanoi's house (front row second from right). Attendees included Masaru Yoshitomi (formerly at Economic Planning Agency, front row far left); Ken'ichi Kōyama (former chair Zengakuren, became professor at Gakushūin University, front row far right); Yasuo Takeuchi (professor at Seijō University, front row second from left); and Kōji Ikuta (back row far right).

Kōji Ikuta, who had entered graduate school a year before me, and I, along with some others, studied modern economics on our own. I was curious to see if there was something new there. When I wasn't able to understand something, if I asked Kōichi Hamada (now professor at Yale University), a year my senior and of the pure modern economics school, I was able to get a clear answer.

As I was looking into this and that, I came across an article that would decisively influence my later research direction. This was an article by Kenneth Arrow and Leonid Hurwicz titled "Decentralization and Computation in Resource Allocation."[1] In this article, the two professors demonstrate that the "gradient method" program-

[1] Arrow, K. J. and L. Hurwicz, "Decentralization and Computation in Resource Allocation," in Pfouts, R. W. (ed.), *Essays in Economics and Econometrics*, University of North Carolina Press, 1960.

M. Aoki, *Transboundary Game of Life*,
https://doi.org/10.1007/978-981-13-2757-5_13

Fig. 13.1 Members of the Tamanoi seminar (author is rear row, far left)

ming they developed to calculate optimal resource allocation was structurally the same shape as the price mechanism. This meant that the market mechanism could be analogous to the working of a large-scale computer solving the problem of economic efficiency. The efficiency that was impossible to attain by centralized planned economies due to limitations of computing power and ability to gather information could be attained compatibly by decentralized market mechanisms and people's incentives. Having been critical of the centralization of the Soviet planned economic state from my early days in the student movement, this proof of the possibility of decentralized economies was truly enlightening.

In retrospect, the twentieth century was one of a world-wide struggle between the options of communism (centralized planned economies) and capitalism (democracy and market economies). It did not stop at that as in mid-century the capitalist economies of the U.S., Germany, and Japan became managed by government controls to a greater or lesser degree. With this as background of that period, the famous dispute in the history of economics over "the possibility of socialist planned economies" arose in the mid-twentieth century. On one side, free economy scholars like Ludwig von Mises and Friedrich A. Hayek argued that in socialist economies where capital goods are nationalized the market for capital goods does not exist, making rational economic calculations impossible. On the other side, the socialist Oskar Lange, who later served as Poland's Ambassador to the United Nations, retorted that economic calculations can be made possible under socialism by having the government mimic market movements.

It is not inconceivable to interpret the work of Arrow and Hurwicz as drawing from this discourse and providing solid formal proof for Lange's ideas. Yet, the conclusion is clear, if we consider whether the administrative bureaucrats in socialist economies have the will or ability to implement Lange's idea, or whether corporations and consumers have the motivation to release information considered reliably necessary. These factors are difficult to implement. Even if the spontaneous market economy is not the optimal system, the socialist planned economy is not any better. This dispute was resolved in practice by the end of the twentieth century. The article by Arrow and Hurwicz presented a systematic, theoretical framework and methodology to think about the problem of system choice.

Of course many conditions are necessary for market mechanisms to be able efficiently to solve the problem of resource allocation in society, even if we leave aside the distribution problem. One of my research topics later became how to allocate resources when those conditions are not met. My encounter with this article by these two economics professors made such an impact on me as to be a revelation. The identification of the most basic issues related to social organization combined with lucid logic—this was what I needed, as I had lost interest in illogical and factional political struggles.

As I studied their works further, I came to understand that Professors Arrow and Hurwicz did not think of social selection through market mechanisms and voting as absolute "given conditions" as other neo-classical economists (such as Samuelson) thought, but rather they were attempting a logical pursuit of arguments considering "variables of selection." This encounter with their article supported me to outgrow Marxism and shift to mathematical economics that incorporated comparative system analysis; and they became my "intellectual" heroes. Professor Arrow was awarded the Nobel Prize in Economics in 1972, and Professor Hurwicz received the National Medal of Science in 1990 and the Nobel Prize in Economics in 2007.

As Ikuta and I studied works on the frontier of theoretical economics and mathematical economics on our own with a few others, an American scholar came as a Fulbright guest professor, something rare for the Faculty of Economics at University of Tokyo. I heard he was looking for an assistant to process data on Japanese labor economy; thinking it might help me study English, I took on this part time job. Amazingly, Professor John Buttrick had come from the University of Minnesota Department of Economics, where Professor Hurwicz taught. In China there is a proverb, "Speak of Cao Cao and Cao Cao arrives" (equivalent to "speak of the devil, and he arrives"). I had received a revelation from reading Professor Hurwicz's article, and now a close colleague of his had appeared before me.

Chapter 14
Operation Study Abroad

"You were in the Zengakuren that turned away Eisenhower?"

In 1963, my second year of graduate school, Professor John Buttrick, who had come from University of Minnesota as a guest professor, asked me, his eyes wide with wonder. The name Zengakuren had gained notoriety in the U.S. His ancestor was Major John Buttrick, one of those who gave the order to "Fire!" on the British forces in Concord, on the outskirts of Boston, starting the American War of Independence in 1775. Having this republican heritage, he was a conscientious objector during World War II and a strong pacifist.

Buttrick specialized in growth theory, but when he found out that I was interested in the mathematical economist Hurwicz's economic mechanism design theory, he urged me to go to University of Minnesota and study under him. Buttrick wrote me a strong letter of recommendation; for a second recommendation letter he suggested that I ask Takashi Negishi (later Chair of the Faculty of Economics), who had returned from studying at Stanford University and had just come to University of Tokyo's Faculty of Economics as a lecturer.

As I was later on the admissions committee for the graduate school in economics at Stanford University, I know that the most important parts of an application are the letters of recommendation and the applicant's essay. The often-used practice in Japan of having the applicant write the recommendation and asking the professor or boss sign it can be seen right through and is not effective. Negishi was diffident as he was a mere lecturer, and had just become one at that. But he was already well-regarded in the U.S. as a mathematical economist and the perfect person to write a recommendation for me.

Thanks to this effort, I was admitted with an assistant's stipend, but things don't go so smoothly in my life. First of all, I was still under my probation sentence, so I needed permission from the court to leave the country. I was concerned, but when I went to request permission from the chief judge at the Tokyo district court, he encouraged me without any problem, saying, "Go and study hard."

The American side was the tricky part. Immigration law states that those who are current or past members of political organizations advocating violent overthrow of

M. Aoki, *Transboundary Game of Life*,
https://doi.org/10.1007/978-981-13-2757-5_14

the government are not allowed entry into the country. This policy was a product of McCarthyism's anti-communism. The exception was with the permission of the Attorney General upon recommendation of the Secretary of State. I figured, even if I could hide my past and go to study abroad, if I get found out, it would be bad, so I decided to make a frontal attack.

When I told the officer at the American Embassy who interviewed me, "I was a participant in an organization called the Bund," he was taken aback. Fortunately, the assistant to then Ambassador to Japan Edwin Reischauer was in the midst of writing a doctoral thesis on Japan's student movement. This was George Packard, who later played an important role in intellectual exchanges between Japan and the U.S. (former President of International University of Japan). I was introduced to him and, perhaps because he was interested because of his studies, he listened to my story.

What I used as my way to make my case was that the Bund and the Zengakuren did not have as their goal anti-Americanism, but rather we were opposed to the resurrection of Japan's militarism, a position that wasn't altogether false. In Yumiko Kurahashi's novel *Seishōjo* (Divine Maiden), there is an episode of some graduate students who had been involved in the anti-Security Treaty movement attempting to go to the U.S. to study mathematical economics. When the main character said he and others had been in fierce opposition and were anti-Yoyogi (where the Japanese Communist Party was headquartered), the official took it that they were anti-communist, and were seen as patriots, a self-serving twist to the argument. Friends of mine teased me that the model for that scene was me, Aoki. But I was dead serious in my negotiations.

During the summer when Tokyo was in the throes of frenzied construction of Olympics facilities, and I was making frequent trips to the American Embassy, Buttrick often invited me to dinner at his house after work. Behind his house lived the artist Santarō Tanabe, and his studio was where a neo-Dadaist artists' group full of energy gathered to drink *shōchū*, cheap white liquor, and danced around naked. With the likely encouragement of Buttrick, Santarō and Ushio Shinohara, another artist, went to New York around the time I went to the U.S. Soon Shinohara decorated a show window on Fifth Avenue with a richly colored object of a courtesan riding a motor cycle, which left even New Yorkers flabbergasted. Santarō became indispensable for the restoration of antique Oriental artworks at the Rockefeller residence and at the White House. Whenever I go to New York, I always visit Santarō's studio in the middle of Manhattan. For the past several decades I have looked forward to going with him to galleries and art dealers to sample New York's art scene.

Just after the dissolution of the Soviet Union, I went to give a lecture at a university in Saint Petersburg, which had just been renamed from Leningrad to its pre-revolutionary name. I bought a splendid miniature icon painting from a young man on the street. It looked to have been forcibly ripped off the wall of a church, perhaps during the turmoil in Russia. Santarō masterfully restored it for me. Despite his failing eyesight which made it difficult for him to draw small paintings, although he could still do dynamic action paintings, Shinohara drew the painting titled 'Pro-

Fig. 14.1 'Professor Aoki at University' by Ushio Shinohara

fessor Aoki at University' (Fig. 14.1) especially for this book.[1] I feel blessed by such extravagance, which is due to my initial meeting with them through Professor Buttrick. As I was preparing for the newspaper serialization of this memoir, Buttrick met with an automobile accident and died in Canada, considered the country to defect to since the Vietnam War days. The photo shown here is one that his widow found a file of his and sent to me (Fig. 14.2).

My visa finally came through at the end of the summer. Some twenty friends from the Bund days, including Shigeo Shima, Kōji Ikuta, Kentarō Karōji, and Susumu Nishibe came to see me off at Haneda Airport. It was the spot where, four years before, we had all been arrested. But each of us kept that thought to ourselves. I bade farewell to the former Bund group who were yelling cheers to me from the rooftop of the airport terminal, and walked up the stairs to the airplane. I was filled with the feeling that a new game of life was beginning for me.

[1] This painting was used as the internal cover of the original Japanese language edition of this book.

Fig. 14.2 With Professor Buttrick, at Katsura Detached Imperial Palace (*photo* by Ann Buttrick)

Chapter 15
To University of Minnesota

I was twenty-six years old when I flew to America to enter the graduate school at University of Minnesota. I landed in San Francisco and stayed at the shabby YMCA on a street lined with bars catering to seamen. When I walked out at night, the strong wind blew old newspapers high into the sky. A sailor who was obviously from the countryside asked me directions. I was enveloped by a sense of liberation that "no one here knows my past," and a pleasant tension that "there is no one I can lean on from now on." I had experienced various twists and turns, but now I had been given the chance to reset my life in America. I felt that I had touched deep in my heart the unfathomable, frightening quality of this country of America. The next day was full of California's sunshine. My mood turned completely optimistic.

I boarded the trans-continental train for Chicago, and first got off in Colorado. I was to have attended a two-month program on economics and English at University of Colorado, supported by the American Economic Association. But my visa problem caused my departure from Japan to be significantly delayed. I thought it would be rude to join the program in the middle, but I decided to follow Buttrick's advice that "It's a wonderful place, so go for even the last few days and have fun."

I passed the final exam in economics with no problem. The professor who taught that course invited me to a barbeque dinner at his house. I remember that there was an insolent ten-year-old boy at the house. That boy was Lawrence Summers who later became the Treasury Secretary and was forced out of his presidency at Harvard University, in part due to discriminatory remarks about academic abilities of women. As for the all-important English marks, the teacher told me, "You can speak English, so you should be all right." This must have been the result of being assistant to Buttrick and attending English language classes at Yotsuya English Academy in the evenings.

Boarding the trans-continental train once more, I went to visit Professor Hirofumi Uzawa at University of Chicago. I was nervous as he was one of my scholarly heroes, along with Arrow and Hurwicz. He treated me to a steak dinner, and as he wanted to buy some gifts to take back to Japan, I accompanied him to a department store. We hardly talked at all about economics, and forgetting about his shopping, he criticized

M. Aoki, *Transboundary Game of Life*,
https://doi.org/10.1007/978-981-13-2757-5_15

America's bombing in the Gulf of Tonkin that led to the intensification of the Vietnam War. When we looked around us, we were surprised to find ourselves walking around in the ladies' lingerie section.

After these stops, I boarded the train that went along the Mississippi River to Minneapolis. In the dining car, the elderly African-American waiter couldn't understand what I ordered. And I couldn't understand what he was saying. An elderly Caucasian woman sitting at the same table translated from English to English, and I was finally able to eat my meal. I became doubtful about the guarantee I received in Colorado for my English ability.

It was September when I arrived in Minneapolis. In those days, Minnesota was known to Japanese only as the land of "The Minnesota Egg Seller," sung by Teruko Akatsuki in the first Kōhaku Uta Gassen, the NHK year-end concert, in 1951. The upbeat song is about a farmer's daughter who sells eggs. People who didn't know why I had chosen to go to Minnesota wondered why I was going to such a rural place rather than to an Ivy League school, which made me feel rather dejected. Indeed, when I got to Minneapolis, I found it to be a "calm" landscape, so different from Tokyo's clamor and dynamism. Invited to dinner at the host family arranged for me by the university, there was quite a culture gap evident in their question, "Do you have television in Japan?" When I retorted, "We also have subways," I must have been expressing my still naïve patriotism.

Classes had not yet begun at the university, so I went to Dinkytown near campus, which Buttrick had told me about, hoping to soak up some of the local atmosphere. He had told me I could hear folk music and jazz at a coffee house named Ten O'Clock Scholar. But I couldn't find it as I searched the two to three block area. I was told it had burned down in a fire six months before. Amazingly, this was where Robert Zimmerman, a student at University of Minnesota until a few years before, had first used his stage name Bob Dylan and played his music. In Dylan's memoir *Chronicles* he depicts in a lively way the musical and poetic influence he received in Dinkytown. Wondering if Buttrick had heard Dylan in his early days, I was filled with envy.

When the academic year started, I went right away to Professor Hurwicz's office to ask for advice. He told me to "study mathematics thoroughly during the first year," and suggested that I take courses from this and that professor who were good at teaching. And that these professors will correct daily assignments and return them to students. In later years, I realized that what Professor Hurwicz meant was that it was more important to get training in logical ways of thinking rather than learning mathematical techniques. In fact, while Hurwicz himself could work out in his head (probably diagrammatically) complex infinite dimension analyses, he wasn't that adept at simple arithmetic such as factoring. As my ideas tend to come in images, the mathematics courses were excellent training for me.

As autumn deepened, I became withdrawn in my room for the first time since my time in Sugamo Prison. I bought a small television set to watch the Tokyo Olympics, but other than the opening ceremony, I couldn't watch much else. In winter, the temperature outside reached 20° below freezing on some days. I crossed a wooden bridge over the Mississippi River every day to go between my dormitory and class. Ice fog rose from the frozen river, and my nose hairs would become frosty. It was like being inside a refrigerator. In summer 2007, there was a news report about a bridge that had collapsed in Minneapolis, causing a dozen or more cars to fall into the river. This was the bridge that was later built next to the bridge I had walked across so many times. One of the reasons given for the collapse was the great range of temperature, which I can certainly vouch for.

There was a restriction on currency exchange, so I had no money sent to me from home. With only a poor graduate assistant stipend, I didn't have money to buy a car. As I had wanted to immerse myself in my studies, this was an ideal environment.

I took a course on mathematical economics from Professor Hurwicz. He aimed to give "lectures that even a horse could understand." He explained difficult theorems by drawing diagrams on the blackboard with many different colors of chalk. Any scholar can explain difficult concepts in a difficult manner, but it is difficult to explain difficult concepts in a simple way. At times he invited me to dinner at his house after giving me advice in his office.

Professor Hurwicz was from Poland, and once at dinner I brought up "Ashes and Diamonds," a film by Andrzej Wajda that I liked. This Polish film is a subtle criticism of the Soviet Union, depicted in the anti-leftist movement youths whose fate is tossed about by the various events from the failure of the uprising against the German occupying forces in Warsaw during World War II to the eve of the communist revolution. The nihilistic style of the main character was popular among our Bund activists. But Professor Hurwicz spat out, "I can't think that Polish people can make a good movie." Mrs. Hurwicz reproached him and told me, "Just because we came from Poland doesn't mean that we like Poland." Being Jewish, Professor Hurwicz was not allowed to sit on a chair in the classroom at his university in Warsaw. He also said that only two of his grade school classmates survived the war.

Professor Hurwicz was in Moscow in 1917 with his family, who had escaped from the invading German forces. He said they knew nothing of what was occurring in the capital, St. Petersburg. I thought that he was so deep in his studies that he didn't even realize that a revolution had occurred; but the point of the joke was that he was a baby at the time. So in 2007 he was ninety years old (Fig. 15.1). I wrote in this series of newspaper articles that among mathematical economists and institutional economists the topic often came up that Hurwicz not yet receiving the Nobel Prize made us doubt the judgment of the selection committee and that he may have lost his chance to be awarded. The evening of October 15, 2007, I arrived at my apartment in Tokyo from San Francisco and finished proofreading my article for the following day. Two hours later, after finishing dinner and thinking I would go to bed as I was jet lagged, a telephone call from the newspaper editor informed me of the news that Hurwicz had been awarded the Nobel Prize. I had just enough time to rewrite the last paragraph of my article before the newspaper went to press. I gave my rewrites over the telephone, and opened a bottle of champagne to toast the occasion with my wife. The next morning, someone told me, "That was writing a live memoir piece, wasn't it?"

ECONOMICS

FALL 2007

GRADUATE ALUMNI NEWSLETTER

Leo Hurwicz Turns 90

On Saturday April 14, 2007 the department hosted a 90th birthday celebration for Leo Hurwicz in the form of a conference and dinner. Entitled "Perspectives on Leo Hurwicz," the event was attended by many colleagues, family, friends, and former advisees. One hundred people came from near and far--as far away as China, Japan and Spain. Held at the Holiday Inn near the West Bank campus, the event started at 1:45pm with opening remarks by University Provost Thomas Sullivan. Sean McDaniels, representing the State of Minnesota, delivered two proclamations by the Governor and the State House declaring April 14th to be "Leo Hurwicz Day." The program then commenced with half-hour talks, beginning with Kenneth Arrow from Stanford, who spoke on "Limited Communication and the Allocation of Labor," followed by Stanley Reiter from Northwestern, "Remarks on Leo Hurwicz's Work on Mechanism Design." After a break, Jim Jordan from Penn State presented "The Communication Required for Convergence of Equilibrium in Economies and Games," and then Daniel McFadden from Berkeley ended the program with "The Human Side of Mechanism Design." All the speakers emphasized Leo's immense contributions to mechanism design. (And, just last year Designing Economic Mechanisms, by Leo and Stan Reiter was published by Cambridge University Press.)

After a cocktail hour, dinner was held, followed by additional speakers. **Dan McFadden** ('62) started off the dinner with a toast to Leo:

"I would like to raise a toast to Leo on behalf of all his former students. Your reputation for placing economics and social science on a rigorous foundation attracted us to the discipline and gave us an appreciation of careful mathematical analysis that threads through and ties together all of economics.

We learned from you that stating and proving theorems is a participatory activity, not a spectator sport. And, you've vaccinated us for life against the modern disease of showing how clever you are by doing economics without a safety net.

Leo, you have one of the longest resumes in economics, once you add to it all of your students who have prospered on your training and ideas. Thank you."

The emcee for the dinner was Ket Richter. Ket also gave an interesting history timeline of Leo's life, noting that, "Leo was born before the Communist regime, outlasted it and is still going strong." To hear Ket's wonderful tribute with all the amazing details, go to http://www.econ.umn.edu/hurwicz and click on "Pictures;" the video clip is then at the top of that next page.

Hugo Sonnenschein, former Minnesota professor, former President of the University of Chicago, and now Professor Emeritus at Chicago, spoke next. Leo helped to hire him in 1964 as an assistant professor on his NSF grant. Hugo

Continued next page .....

Fig. 15.1 University of Minnesota alumni magazine article on Hurwicz turning 90

It was certainly something to celebrate. But Professor Hurwicz's health wasn't up to going to Stockholm to accept the Nobel Prize in Economics. The Swedish Ambassador went to University of Minnesota to hold the award ceremony at the same time as the one held in Sweden. This was streamed over the Internet.

Chapter 16
Job Market

As I had studied quite a bit at University of Tokyo graduate school, I was able to complete my required courses during my first year at University of Minnesota in good order. This allowed me to look forward to summer vacation of 1965 with a sense of freedom. I had some unexpected good fortune that summer. Professor Hirofumi Uzawa at University of Chicago allowed me to join a workshop that he held for several outstanding graduate students from Massachusetts Institute of Technology (MIT). At that time Professor Uzawa was conducting joint research with Professor Hurwicz on the difficult problem of mathematically deriving demand function from utility function. He visited Minnesota occasionally to work on this joint project.

At this workshop, the students presented their doctoral thesis ideas one at a time and everyone discussed them. In the evening we all went to a beer hall. Among this group were Joseph E. Stiglitz and George Akerlof.[1] They were still in their mid-twenties, but they were already discussing the idea of the theory of "asymmetric information," which later led to the research for which they were awarded the Nobel Prize.

Mrs. Uzawa was in Japan that summer, so Prof. Uzawa and I experimented how to make tempura in the kitchen of his apartment and fed everyone. Even now Stiglitz says, "That tempura tasted so good."

At the end of the summer I went to the West Coast to get married (Fig. 16.1). When I had fled the frontlines after the 1960 anti-Security Treaty struggle, I had gotten to know an actress in the Mingei Theater group, and we had become engaged. The reason we hadn't married right away was because she was troubled as to whether she should give up her career as an actress. Our wedding was just the two of us going to San Francisco City Hall and making our pledge before the justice of the peace. In repeating what the justice said, as he pronounced 'Aoki' sounding like 'Aye-oki,' I

[1] I served as President of the International Economic Association (IEA) for three years from 2008, when the vice committee chair was Eytan Sheshinski of Israel's Hebrew University; and the following President was Joseph Stiglitz. All of us were products of the small group in the Uzawa seminar.

M. Aoki, *Transboundary Game of Life*,
https://doi.org/10.1007/978-981-13-2757-5_16

Fig. 16.1 Summer 1965, at Berkeley (27 years old)

parroted back to him that same pronunciation. Professor Ryūtarō Komiya, who was a guest professor at Stanford University, and his wife hosted a celebratory party for us.

In my second year, Professor Hurwicz suddenly went to India as a guest professor. This meant I would write my doctoral thesis under Professor John Chipman. In my third year Professor Chipman went to Harvard University as a guest professor. So I went to Harvard, although still enrolled at University of Minnesota, to finish my thesis there. My topic was what kind of tax and subsidy policies should be employed to the economy overall in the case of pollution, an external factor. I approached this from a general equilibrium theory.

At American universities, when one is close to obtaining one's doctorate, one enters the job market to look for an assistant professorship. In recent years several hundred students planning to complete their doctorates gather from around the country to attend the annual meeting of the American Economic Association held in early January each year. There they can be interviewed by economics departments interested in hiring them. Some students boast that they interviewed with twenty top-ranked universities, while some are dejected at not getting even one chance to interview. At Stanford University, we split up the process and interview several dozen candidates. From them we select about ten and invite them to give talks at university seminars; and finally we make concrete offers (with salaries and such conditions to indicate our intention to hire).

At this stage, it becomes a seller's market, with a bidding war developing among major universities for popular student candidates. The candidates are not all Americans, but come from various countries. The high quality of American universities is supported in part by this competitive market system. I understand that recently University of Tokyo's Faculty of Economics participates in this sort of market, with some success in hiring assistant professors, which is needed in order to increase internationalization and improve quality of research.

When I entered the job market, however, there was only a small supply of mathematical economics graduate students, and the market hadn't become institutionalized as it is now. When my advisor Professor Chipman sent a letter to a university he thought might be possible for me, there would be an immediate invitation to give a seminar there. Being a scatterbrain, I had some goofs such as mistaking the day for the job talk, causing the university to hold an ad hoc seminar for me, something that would be unthinkable now.

Professor Wassily Leontief, whom I worked for as a research assistant, looked favorably on me and said, "Stay at Harvard." But his field was empirical input-output analysis, and differed from my interest in mathematical economics. The place I wanted to go to was Stanford University, where Kenneth Arrow, whom I had looked on as a hero along with Hurwicz since my extra years at University of Tokyo, taught. As fate would have it, Arrow was at MIT, just a stone's throw away from Harvard, as a guest professor at that time. I was interviewed in his office. When I described my thesis idea, with his speedy thought process, said to be like a calculator, he immediately understood the content of my analysis, and told me, "Stanford will probably make an offer." He asked me "What kind of offer do you have from other universities?" I told him about $10,000 in salary, he was astonished as his starting salary some ten years before had been $3000. A week or so later, I received the actual offer for an assistant professorship from the Economics Department. Other universities called me and made competing offers.

I was faced with a difficult choice amidst this abundance of fortune. This is because Arrow himself was fielding offers from Harvard and MIT. When I asked him, "What do you plan to do?" He answered, "I haven't made a decision yet, but I will be at Stanford for the next year, so why don't you come?" The charm of the tranquil town of Cambridge, where Harvard is located, was difficult to resist as a place to live. Though Harvard was then weak in mathematical economics, if Arrow were to settle there, the situation would make an about turn. But Arrow was known for his loyalty to Stanford, and there was no guarantee that he would accept an offer from politically conservative Harvard. I wrestled with my choices, while both Harvard and Stanford pressured me to make up my mind. I followed Arrow's suggestion and made the decision to go to Stanford. One week later, Arrow made his decision to go to Harvard a year later. It wasn't that Arrow had meant to mislead me. But this turn of events gave me a greater shock than my failures in the entrance exams for Shōnan High School and University of Tokyo graduate school.

This happened when I was about to turn twenty-nine. As I will note later, my decision at that time ultimately led to a happy relationship with Arrow and with Stanford that continues to this day. One can never tell what life will bring.

Chapter 17
Serra House

In the summer of 1967 I left the sedate streets of New England lined with brick buildings and traveled across the North American continent, headed for California, with its bright blue skies, to take up the post of assistant professor at Stanford University. My mode of transportation was a Volvo, what was then considered the safest automobile. It was a time when Japanese cars were still not considered reliable on the highways. Counting on my annual salary as assistant professor, which was an increase several times over from my stipend as a graduate student research assistant, I spent money to buy a new car. But this was a bit lacking in foresight, as I later found it a burden to pay off the monthly car loan. Driving about 500 miles a day, I enjoyed taking about a week to cross the country. On an upward slope in the Colorado mountains, the car's engine conked out, perhaps due to lack of oxygen, and it was a thrill to restart the engine by rolling the car backwards downhill.

At Stanford, my office was located in Serra House, formerly the university president's residence in a eucalyptus grove. Professor Kenneth Arrow, who was in charge of the sacred ground of mathematical economics, whose rare accomplishments would later earn him a Nobel Prize at the young age of 51, had an analytic ability of lightning speed, a warm heart, and sharp concern for society, wide-ranging knowledge and a retentive memory. He was a top-flight scholar in all respects around whom gathered brilliant young researchers from the world over. Taking just the Japanese who were former members of the Serra House group, there were illustrious professors including: Hirofumi Uzawa, Michio Morishima, Ken'ichi Inada, Takashi Negishi, and Yasusuke Murakami (Fig. 17.1).

I spent an academically productive year at this research institute, blessed by colleagues including: Mordecai Kurz, Ken'ichi Inada, T.N. Srinivasan, and Lawrence Lau. Serra House had been, after all, a residence, which made it seem as if we were at a vacation house as we focused on research. At lunch time we would get into a car together to go to eat sandwiches. It was a very congenial atmosphere. When British and French forces bombed Egypt, though, there was a furious argument between Kurz, who was Israeli, and Srinivasan, who was a left-leaning Indian.

M. Aoki, *Transboundary Game of Life*,
https://doi.org/10.1007/978-981-13-2757-5_17

Fig. 17.1 Colleagues at Serra House (author at far left, Prof. Arrow second from right)

A special memory I have is forming a life-long friendship with Janos Kornai (Professor Emeritus at Harvard University), who occupied the office next to mine at Serra House. In *Overcentralization in Economic Administration*, his book based on his experience as a journalist for the Hungarian Communist Party newspaper, he made pertinent criticisms of problem areas in socialist economies. In the 1956 Hungarian Uprising he was driven out of the Communist Party and was confined to a research institute in the countryside. Arrow had invited him at that time.

Kornai and I were pursuing similar ways of thinking about our academic research. This was a mathematical problem of what mechanism could effect efficient resource allocation where there are externalities and economies of scale, in an environment where the price mechanism dealt with by Arrow and Hurwicz doesn't work. Kornai began to consider this within the framework of socialist planned economies, while as I later developed my ideas this became the theoretical basis for the role of corporate organizations in market economies. Kornai was starting to write what became *Anti-Equilibrium*, a pioneering work critiquing neo-classical economics. He secretly showed me his manuscript, which was to swell to five times in volume, but he was hesitant to show it to Arrow, a leading proponent of neo-classical economics. For his part, Arrow was to go beyond market fundamentalism, and was about to prepare a ground-breaking article suggesting the promotion of the economics of health care.

Both Kornai and I had fought ideological battles against the Communist Party in our own countries, but in the U.S., we were on the immigration law's "blacklist," and shared a constant worry about our visas. Shortly after I began working at Stanford, I received in my mailbox at home a document ordering my deportation. The reason was that my "purpose of study in graduate school had been accomplished." This was a shock to me. But thanks to the Democratic economists Arrow, Kenneth Galbraith, Leontief, and Walter Heller (University of Minnesota professor who had been the chair of the Council of Economic Advisers during the Kennedy administration) who wrote letters to the economist W.W. Rostow, then Special Assistant for National Security Affairs, I was able to continue in my post of assistant professor at Stanford University.

Years later, as it had become a nuisance to obtain permission from the U.S. Attorney General each time I departed from the U.S., I applied for a Green Card for permanent residency in 1993. Normally, one isn't allowed to leave the U.S. while waiting for the Green Card to be issued. I was invited to attend a United Nations meeting in Africa, and received my permanent residency very quickly. In Africa, I felt outrage at the U.N. officials and advisers fattening their own wallets, and protested this situation. My ally in this effort was Lo Fu-chen, then the Deputy Director of the United Nations University Institute of Advanced Studies in Japan. I learned that at University of Pennsylvania graduate school, he was a close friend of Kōji Ikuta, with whom I had traveled the same intellectual path of student movement, Uno economics, modern economics, and study abroad in the U.S.

Ikuta had come to the U.S. a year after me, and he sent me a postcard when I was in Minnesota in the spring of 1968, saying in his typical way, "I'm going to trundle my car there to see you." Just after that, he and his wife died in a fire in their apartment building. Dr. Lo took their ashes back to Japan, to the temple run by Saeki's family, where we had joined in many discussions (see Chap. 3: Three Influential Seniors).

While studying in the U.S., Dr. Lo became an activist in the Taiwan independence movement. After retiring from the U.N. University, he packed up his belongings and returned to Taiwan. Before he could unpack, he was appointed by President Chen Shui-bian as Representative of the Taipei Economic and Cultural Representative Office in Tokyo, equivalent to ambassadorial rank, and returned to Japan. He would invite me to dinner when mutual acquaintances from his University of Pennsylvania days visited Japan. The name he took for his calligraphic work decorating the dining room of his official residence in Shirogane, Tokyo, included one of the characters in Kōji Ikuta's name.

Why did Ikuta have to die in such a freak accident? Was it because he had led such a condensed life? I am convinced that if he were alive now we would have become the strongest of comrades in pioneering the field of comparative institutional analysis. His death leaves me full of remorse.

Chapter 18
Counterculture

The area around Stanford University was later to be called Silicon Valley, the cradle of high tech start-up companies. But in 1967, when I first lived there, there were fruit orchards just a step away from El Camino Real ("The King's Way"), the main old road from Stanford to San Jose. Leading IT industry companies like Apple, Sun Microsystems, Cisco, and Google did not even exist in this world. The headquarters and offices of these companies were built on these orchard lands and San Francisco Bay landfill.

In this peaceful residential area where stories of Hewlett Packard being founded in a garage and Steve Jobs building the first Apple computer by hand in his father's living room, there were signs of the birth of another movement in the Bay Area. This was the counterculture of rock music, drugs, hippies, and anti-Vietnam war movement.

Among businessmen and engineers now in their 50s and 60s who were involved in the creation of Silicon Valley, many of them were baptized by the counterculture in one way or another, whether they were hippies in their youth, or rock music fans. This is not strange, as this movement rebelled against old-fashioned American mass consumerism, hierarchical organizational culture, and machine civilization that replaced human bodies.

An article discussing the social meaning of this counterculture appeared in "New Music Magazine" (now "Music Magazine"), a monthly that began publication in 1969. Along with Tōru Takemitsu, a leading Japanese composer, Namito Yabe wrote an article on "Rock in America's cultural revolution." This piece garnered some attention, and was actually written by me, as I observed close-hand the counterculture movement of the time. The pen name I chose came from the characters for my mentor in economics, Arrow (ya), and the tribal lifestyle of the counterculture (be); I took Namito (wave person) from the clarinetist George Lewis's jazz tune "Over the Waves" which I had been a fan of since university days (Fig. 18.1).

M. Aoki, *Transboundary Game of Life*,
https://doi.org/10.1007/978-981-13-2757-5_18

Fig. 18.1 New Music Magazine, Number 6, September 1969

It was a time when the legendary rock singer Janis Joplin and the Grateful Dead performed free concerts in a park near Stanford. Joan Baez, called the queen of folk songs, was the daughter of a Stanford University professor. While she was in high school, she had made Kepler's, the nearby bookstore, her base of operations, and she married a leader of Stanford University's anti-war movement. My pop music record collection was the object of envy of my daughters' generation, when they were in high school in the late 1990s.

A year later, I left California, the breeding ground of this new culture, and once again drove across the country in the Volvo. This was because Arrow was moving from Stanford to Harvard, and some of us young researchers, including myself, made a tribal migration. Harvard resurrected its previous year's offer to me.

On the East Coast, to which I had returned after a year, the counterculture had burst forth in a more political manner. The student movement opposing the Vietnam War had become increasingly radicalized. In the spring of 1969, several hundred ultra-radical students occupied the Harvard College deans' offices and pulled out classified documents related to military research contracts from filing cabinets to expose them. The university called in the police force to evict the students. In Harvard Yard, students countered by throwing rocks at the police, in an unprecedented incident. Moderate students rapidly became politicized. An all-university meeting attended by 10,000 people was held at the university football stadium, which I hadn't set foot in until then, and a strike was voted on. The conservative dean was forced to take a leave.

At the protest meetings in Harvard Yard, with its several hundred years of history, rock bands played, and architecture students made pop art strike posters and silkscreened T-shirts. I felt a sense of déjà vu. It was the same kind of festive atmosphere that I had experienced some ten years earlier at Japan's Diet Building. I wondered about the meaning of this melding of the political anti-war protest and cultural revolution movement. A decade earlier in Japan the "music biker gang" of Masaaki Hirao and others (Chap. 8: Middle School Years) and the "red biker gang" of the Zengakuren had not combined directly. I wrote in an article immediately after this Harvard disturbance which included the following comments.

"When a movement breaks out from the framework of solely being political and youths seek an expansion of their spirit within the act of participating in the movement, it is natural for rock music and the new left to merge. This is because, unlike folk songs that essentially read poems, rock pursues the ultimate limits of the natural voice and is a potent 'full body experience.' If folk's true nature was to send a message to others, rock's message is self-liberation."[1] My article is high-minded, reflecting the spirit of the times swirling around the campus. However, having experienced the discouragement after the festival-like excitement of the anti-Security Treaty struggle, I couldn't help but continue stating as follows.

"As the true nature of a revolutionary movement is to replace the existing human relationship with a new human relationship, the human relations within the protest movement must reflect the potential of new human relations. If true revolution is to demolish the political ruler/non-ruler relationship, whether there is the sprouting of a communal consciousness and behavior within an anti-establishment movement gives an indication of whether that movement is truly radical. A movement that is solely political, though it may initially succeed, will result in nothing more than creating another authoritarian society." Viewed from this stance that I reached after the anti-Security Treaty protests, I began to feel antagonistic toward the group that pushed for political radicalization after the Harvard Yard disturbance. In exchange, I felt somewhat sympathetic to the style of non-violent protests and the way of life of Ken Kesey and others who were non-political and had begun to experiment with a naturalistic "tribal" communal life.[2]

Rewording my stance in the article with words I use today, I would state it this way. New rules in the social game do not appear suddenly after the old rules are destroyed. They are born from the method of play that has been experimented with

---

[1] When Dylan had made the leap from folk to rock a little while before this time, many people were shocked by his transformation and were unable to go along with it.

[2] Ken Kesey authored *One Flew over the Cuckoo's Nest*, a literary masterpiece on the inhumanity of American society symbolically set in a mental institution, and began living a tribal style of life. It is said that, at his commune, he was attempting to recreate the naturalism of Henry David Thoreau, who had lived a self-sustaining life at Walden Pond outside of Boston in the mid-nineteenth century.

and nurtured among those attempting to change the rules, resulting in their gradual acceptance by the society. After the Harvard Yard disturbance, American society was beset by a dismal period with a great cleavage in society concerning the Vietnam War. In that period, the ever more radicalized political movement lost its influence and died out. But in Silicon Valley, the same place where the cultural revolution occurred, a business culture eventually arose, where small-scale organizations that are non-authoritarian and pursue the making of new things come and go. And many from the anti-Vietnam War generation have participated in this process. This new organizational culture was not something that was born from nothing.

Getting back to the past, there was a time after the inciting incident of the Harvard Yard disturbance, that many young economists and graduate students leaned toward Marxism. While drawing a line between myself and these Marxists late-comers, I became close to the leading proponents Herbert Gintis and Samuel Bowles, who had brilliant minds and a spirit of criticism of the current situation as well as a wealth of humanity. They eventually overcame the internal conflicts inherent in protest movements that I mentioned by distancing themselves from Marxism. Based at Santa Fe Institute and other places, they have developed an evolutionary theory of institutional economics through research from various dimensions, including theory, fieldwork, and experimentation. When I meet them at conferences or summer schools, including those in Italy or Hungary, where there is increasing interest in institutional economics, I am delighted that we have greater chances for discussion over dinner.

When I think about it, there are quite a few scholars with whom I have the privilege of close association who were Marxist-leaning when they were young. These include Janos Kornai; Douglass North, a pioneer of new institutional economics; Nathan Rosenberg, a trailblazer of the economics of technology innovation, and the Chair of the Economics Department when I later returned to Stanford; Gerard Roland, who researches transitional political economics from socialism to market economies; and the late James Abegglen, who was the originator of Japanese management theory. I wonder if Marx's dynamic social perspective was like measles, something to go through to acquire immunity, for scholars who thought about institutional evolution and change in the twentieth century.

Chapter 19
Day of Departure from America

By 1969, the year that Harvard University was embroiled in the student movement, I realized it had been five years since I had left Japan. Not having returned to Japan during that time, the period of high economic growth rate experienced in Japan was entirely missing from my own experience. I received an offer to become an assistant professor at the newly founded Institute of Economic Research at Kyoto University. The late Director Hideo Aoyama and the late Professor Tsunehiko Watabe were engaged in founding a research institute with an excellent research environment. I hadn't yet made up my mind whether to return to Japan, but I thought I could spend one year there and return to Harvard before making a final decision. So I accepted this kind offer.

Arriving in Japan, I saw that the student movement was in full flower. In my past Bund days I had occasionally gone to Kyoto to organize at Kyoto University and Doshisha University. But the actions had become much more radical. The first day that I went to my office at Kyoto University, the wooden front gate that I had passed through in the morning was burned to the ground by the evening. I don't know which sect was responsible for this, but after there had been some rock throwing, a Molotov cocktail had been thrown onto the barricade put up at the gate. The Red Army faction that said they traced themselves to the old Bund telephoned me, having heard that "Himeoka" had returned, but I answered, "We don't have anything in common anymore." The young man's voice was cheerful, and I wonder what happened to him. A while later, in 1972, three gold-colored stars were drawn on the tile roof of Seibu Kōdō, the university clubs' building, located across Higashiyama-dōri avenue across from the Institute of Economic Research. The three stars appeared the morning after three Japanese Red Army members attacked the airport at Tel Aviv.

While I was in Japan, I wrote my first book as a scholar, *Economic Theory of Organization and Planning* (Iwanami Shoten), published in Japanese. This work delineated the outcome of mechanism design theory of that day, stating that price mechanism is insufficient for the effective allocation of economic resources, and that it requires combination with quantitative adjustment by institutions and regulations. For example, in tackling externalities such as pollution, rather than relying on a near

M. Aoki, *Transboundary Game of Life*,
https://doi.org/10.1007/978-981-13-2757-5_19

price mechanism such as environmental tax, it is better to limit the total volume of pollution and fine tune the allocation iteratively. This theory connects to the thinking behind the present-day market for emission right trading. It was a time when the debts from rapid economic growth came due in the form of environmental problems that became a significant socio-political problem, for which modern economics was starting to develop the non-market mechanism theory in the field of public economics. This book received the Nikkei Prize for Economics Books in 1970.

After a year, I went back to Harvard and taught microeconomics at the graduate level with Leontief. I also led a seminar on "comparative mechanism theory" with Professor Hurwicz, my mentor at University of Minnesota. Hurwicz was at Harvard to look it over, as Arrow had given as his condition of accepting Harvard's offer that Hurwicz would also be given an offer. There were only a few attending this seminar, one of whom was Abram Bergson, the authority on Soviet economics and well-known in welfare economics, who participated despite his elderly age. What Hurwicz was beginning to think about at that time, that the designs of economic mechanisms cannot be implemented unless there is compatibility with the hidden incentives of economic agents. This became the research for which he was awarded the Nobel Prize in Economics in 2007.

Among the graduate students was Iwao Nakatani, who was on leave from Nissan Motor Company; and right next door at MIT were Takenori Inoki and Katsuhito Iwai. We continue to get together occasionally with our families for reunions of our "Cambridge Alumni Club." Also at the Harvard-Yenching Institute as visiting scholar was Takehiko Noguchi, who during the anti-Security Treaty days was a leader of the Zenjiren (National Liaison Council of Student Self-governing Associations), the student organization counter to the Bund, unable to break with the Communist Party leadership, even though it was opposed to it. Both of us had left the political movement after the early 1960s, and had gone into the academic world of literature and economics, respectively. The animosity of a decade earlier had disappeared, and while respecting each other's intellectual endeavors, we came to associate on good terms. He had secured a firm place for himself in literary circles with his *The World of Yukio Mishima* (Kōdansha). I recall that after Yukio Mishima had committed ritual suicide, we were in a confused state of shock as we drank deep into the night.

In the Economics Department, the discord between the conservative economists and the radical faction of Gintis and Bowles was exacerbated in the context of the stalemate of the Vietnam War. At a faculty meeting a few years later, tenure was denied to these two who among the assistant professors were outstanding in their popularity, abilities, and human qualities. Only three faculty members voted for giving them tenure: Arrow, Leontief, and Galbraith. These three professors were the ones who supported me when I was given deportation orders from the American government. This tenure vote was an indirect cause of Arrow returning to Stanford and Leontief moving to New York University. Hurwicz also refused Harvard's offer and returned to University of Minnesota.

Under these dismal circumstances I was hit personally with a crushing psychological blow . This was my wife's death by accident. In the fall of 1971, I called home

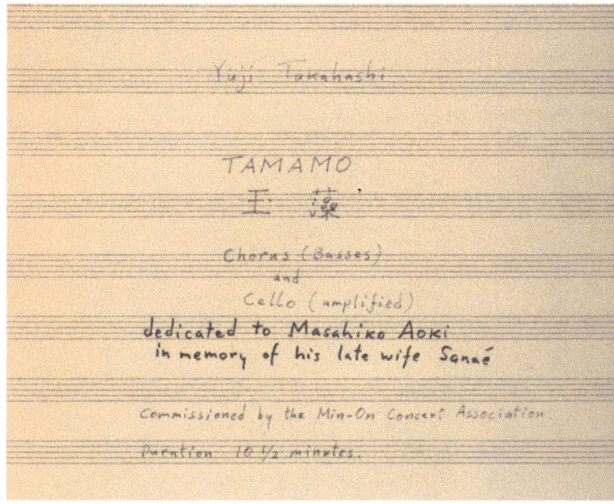

Fig. 19.1 Sheet music for "Tamamo," composed by Yūji Takahashi in memory of my late wife

in the early evening, "I'm heading home now," and left my office. When I reached our apartment on foot some ten minutes later, the house was utterly quiet. It was a wordless farewell.

The Economics Department Chair Henry Rosovsky, though politically conservative, was a very warmhearted person, and he obtained permission from the university to issue the funds for me to take my wife's body back to Japan and gave me two weeks of leave. The composer Yūji Takahashi, my friend from our Shōnan Gakuen middle school days, composed "Tamamo," based on a poem by Hitomaro Kakinomoto in the *Manyōshū*, for cello and chorus, dedicated to my wife's memory (Fig. 19.1). By happenstance, it was a cello player that I later met and married. Mrs. Leontief, a poet, wrote a poem in my wife's memory. My colleagues and students warmly consoled me. In particular, the late Tsuneo Ishikawa, at that time a doctoral student at Johns Hopkins University, who was writing his thesis under Arrow as his advisor, was more attentive than even a brother could have been, and helped me out in many ways. Later, when his doctoral thesis was completed, his achievement was recognized, and he remained at Harvard as an assistant professor, and wrote a noteworthy article with the radical economist Gintis. Some thirty years ago, he collapsed in his office at University of Tokyo, and I was forced to bid farewell to him without being able to see him again.

Having settled things after the unforeseen tragedy, as I walked alone on the streets, stepping on the crackling fallen leaves, I looked down at my feet and was overcome by the unreal feeling that they weren't part of my body.

My mind was made up that my day of departure from America had come.

Chapter 20
Wavering About Economics

In April 1972, the year after I lost my wife, I returned to Kyoto University via London. At the University, the students had gone on a lengthy strike to protest the dismissal by the Faculty of Economics of a radical instructor named Nobuhiro Takemoto, who had gone underground and hadn't appeared on campus. As I was at the Institute of Economic Research, I didn't have lecture duties, but acceding to the wishes of students, I volunteered to give an unofficial seminar (Fig. 20.1). One of the attendees was Mitsuhiro Fukao, an engineering student, who later became a noted economist.

Around that time, Hurwicz, my advisor at University of Minnesota, in his distinguished "Ely Lecture" at the American Economic Association (1972), mentioned my work as being leading-edge research on economic mechanism design. This led to an offer of a contract from a leading academic publisher abroad to publish the English language version of my *Economic Theory of Organization and Planning* (Iwanami Shoten), which I had written in Japanese. But I couldn't get up the motivation to do this. In the end, this book never came out in English, which I now realize was a failure. Why did I feel so withdrawn? From a combination of factors—the Vietnam War, problems of pollution, antagonism between the neo-classical faction and the radical faction, my wife's death by accident—I had begun to waver about abstract mathematical economics.

Fig. 20.1 With students at Kyoto University (author at front left)

M. Aoki, *Transboundary Game of Life*,
https://doi.org/10.1007/978-981-13-2757-5_20

Around this time, I renewed my acquaintance with Susumu Nishibe, with whom I had fled from the front lines of the Bund, who was now teaching economics at the University of Tokyo College of Arts and Sciences. He had gone beyond criticism of neo-classical economics to read extensively books on sociology and linguistics, and had a deep understanding of them. I also gained the opportunity to talk from time to time with Ikutarō Shimizu, a comrade in the Zengakuren, who was a generation before Takaaki Yoshimoto in the anti-Security Treaty struggles, after we held a dialogue for a magazine. This was when he was writing his prominent *Notes on Ethics* (Iwanami Shoten).

While I was at Harvard University, I attended some of the classes given in the early days of phenomenological sociology and associated with the political philosopher John Rawls, who authored *A Theory of Justice*. It was still unclear to me how to reconcile economics, which is based on methodological individualism, and sociology that studies social norms and values. Although it was a time when Samuelson's position that many economists "separate economics from sociology upon the basis of rational or irrational behavior" (*Foundations of Economic Analysis*, 1947, p. 90) was taken for granted, it must have been frustrating for Nishibe and Shimizu, who had readily rejected methodological individualism.

It was a body blow to me that Nishibe criticized as "an anomaly" my naïve patchwork effort at that time to consolidate sociology, economics, and philosophy in his 1975 publication *Socioeconomics* (Chūō Kōron Shinsha). It took twenty years from that time for me to come up with a solution to this problem that was satisfactory.

Nishibe said, "Aoki and I are like hyperbolic curves that come from infinitely far away, and now may be close to each other, but will most likely part again and go off into infinitely far off distances." He was from Hokkaido and I was from the Shōnan beach area; and our family backgrounds were also very different. We got into an argument at the party after my wedding for my second marriage, and broke off our association. As he predicted, we became far distant from each other in our thinking. However, what I studied during that time later bore fruit for me.

I met my present wife at a mutual friend's house. She was a cellist who had just graduated from Tokyo University of the Arts. Nothing ever seems to go smoothly for me, and sure enough, there was a dust up before we could get married. This was because her aunt and other relatives were furiously opposed to me. Her grandfather, Kiichirō Nikaidō was a judge in the appeals court in Miyagi Prefecture in prewar times. In the 1937 Popular Front Incident, when the government sought to suppress political leftists, he had rendered an acquittal of a Marxist (meaning Tohoku University Professor Kōzō Uno of "Uno Economics"). Despite this, when he was later sent to Manchuria to be the assistant director of the judicial bureau, he was killed by a Marxist (meaning the Soviet forces). Their feeling was that Marxists (meaning me) have no understanding of what it means to be obligated, so we can't trust them. It was a syllogism on the order of "if the wind blows, the coffin maker gets rich."

Her father had passed away a few years before we met, but as her mother stood firmly by us, we were able to get married despite opposition from her relatives. We were married on April 27, 1975, two days before the end of the Vietnam War with the complete withdrawal of U.S. troops.

Chapter 21
Visiting Closed China

Although Japan had normalized relations with China in 1972, China was under the control of the "Gang of Four" in the 1970s, and was still firmly closed to the outside world. The actual conditions of the Cultural Revolution were still wrapped in mystery. It could be said that for those interested in the sociology of systems, there was no other country that drew as much curiosity.

Marriage gradually made me feel more positive. As I had seen quite a bit of the U.S., I began to think I would like to see China. Reading *Shanghai Times* (Chūkō Shinsho) by Shigeharu Matsumoto, who was active as a journalist in the prewar period, gave impetus to this idea of mine. He wrote that one reason the Second World War became inevitable was that prewar Japan lacked the vantage point of having a "compound eye" that could see the West and the East simultaneously in its field of vision. The Asianists didn't know about the West, and those who knew about the West neglected China, with the result that neither side was able to cope with Japan's circumstances. I thought this was very perceptive.

China at that time wasn't a country that would easily allow a desire to peek into it from academic curiosity. But I had an heirloom sword I could pull out as a trump card. My father urged me to seek help from Kaheita Okazaki, who was an outside board member of my grandfather's company. As chief representative of the Japan-China Memorandum Trade Office from pre-normalization years, Mr. Okazaki worked to improve relations between Japan and China, and was trusted by Premier Zhou Enlai.

When I went to meet with him in autumn of 1975, he surprised me by saying, "The two people I respect the most in my life are Zhou Enlai and your grandfather, Shūzō Nishihara." It seemed Mr. Okazaki felt a resonance with the devotion that my grandfather had toward developing environmental technology. With that connection, even though my grandfather was deceased, he easily promised to get word to Zhou Enlai on my behalf. Zhou died the following January, but Mr. Okazaki had kept his word.

I invited six young economists who were interested in comparative systems theory and Chinese economy, headed by Katsuji Nakagane (then at Institute of Developing Economies) who was proficient in Chinese. Upon Mr. Okazaki's advice that to

M. Aoki, *Transboundary Game of Life*,
https://doi.org/10.1007/978-981-13-2757-5_21

Fig. 21.1 At Dazhai, with Yukihiko Kiyokawa, then Associate Professor at Hitotsubashi University (right)

understand China it is best to see agricultural villages, we joined a study tour of the Japan-China Agricultural Farmers Friendship Association.

When we landed at Shanghai Airport in March 1976, our suitcases and luggage were loaded up on bicycle-drawn carts. We went on to Dazhai, known for the Communist Party slogan, "Learn from Daqing in industry and from Dazhai in agriculture." It was the legendary model district of the Gang of Four, proclaiming the heroic efforts of the people's commune to bring land under cultivation in spite of the area being in a highland where crops were not easy to grow (Fig. 21.1).

We spent several days there, but without any heating, it was so cold we couldn't sleep without tying our neckties tight so that no air could get in from our necks. We had just one basin of hot water each day. But strangely enough the food was plentiful, and the people's commune leaders always ate with us. The land reclamation was a huge civil engineering operation that went far beyond what could be accomplished by the impoverished farmers' people's commune. We spoke among ourselves that, "Whatever its start, in order to create a model people's commune, they must have had support from the Liberation Army to carry out such a huge reclamation project."

During our trip, we debated on the rights and wrongs of China's nuclear tests with our interpreter who was also monitoring us. The Gang of Four was still in power, and wherever we went, we were isolated from average citizens. Slipping away from the interpreter's monitoring, we went out in the streets to gather information from newspapers posted on walls and from conversations. For this purpose, Nakagane's linguistic ability was an indispensable weapon. The campaign criticizing the "capitalist roader" (reactionary who walks the road of capitalism), who was said to have stated, "It doesn't matter if a cat is white or black, as long as it catches mice," was unfolding without yet naming Deng Xiaoping. But we did not see people crowding around the newspapers posted on walls, and it was clear that the influence of the Gang of Four was on the wane. During our weeks in China, we saw not one dog, either in the countryside or in the cities. This might have been related to food shortages.

On our visit to Tsinghua University, there were no students on campus, only the Liberation Army guarding the library. We met with the University Revolutionary

Committee Chief (acting as University President), Chi Qun. This obviously sharp-minded but overbearing man clearly stated to us, "We will oust Deng Xiaoping soon." That is what happened shortly afterward. About six months later, he himself was arrested along with Jiang Qing and the Gang of Four, and was sentenced to imprisonment. A quarter of a century later, I would visit that same room under an entirely different context. The scholars and administrative officials I became friendly with in the meantime had been "sent down" to the remote countryside.

In the final days of our stay in China, we went to Tiananmen Square where people were gathered in memory of Zhou Enlai, who had passed away several months before. They had brought artificial flowers, red flags, and poems written in ink and brush. They say that this had the intention of implicitly criticizing the leadership of that time, using the Qingming Festival to honor the dead, but the atmosphere was festive. Just after we left, the flowers and poems were swept away overnight by the authorities in the first Tiananmen Incident. Some say there were some victims in this process, but the truth of the matter is not yet known to the outside world.

This visit to a unique place at this unusual time was a very valuable experience for me. I later became involved with China both academically and in terms of policy. Although this trip was short, what I observed provided me with a thoroughly interesting case of the early conditions required for system change.

Chapter 22
Thoughts on Corporations East and West

During my trip to China, I spent time deep in conversation with Iwao Nakatani, my friend from Harvard days, and Masayuki Iwata, a specialist on socialist economics, as we rode the bus to Dazhai, the "agricultural model district." At that time the two of them were researching "labor-managed firms," where the power is held not by stockholders but by the workers. The model for this type of firm originated from Yugoslavian firms, and this theory was being advanced in Europe and the U.S. We talked about how Japanese firms have a workers' authority aspect as well.

Taking a hint from this conversation, I thought up a corporate model of game theory wherein the company owner manages the firm by balancing the benefits to both the stockholders and employees. In this model, the balance between stockholders and laborers in both the traditional neoclassical stockholder-governed firms and the labor-managed firms becomes a special case of one versus zero to one or the other side. This is the foundation for what is now called the stakeholder theory of corporate governance.

When this model was about to be published in *American Economic Review*, Professor Dale Jorgenson, a friend from my Harvard days, invited me to spend the year from 1979 as a Fulbright exchange professor at Harvard. Once again I went to Harvard. At a party at the Jorgensons' house, Professor Harvey Leibenstein, and authority on corporate theory, came toward me and was nice enough to tell me, "That article of yours is good." Spurred on by such comments, I participated in seminars on corporate governance at the Law School between my teaching assignments. This was a time when economists were not yet paying much attention to the importance of corporate governance, in particular the connection between law and economy. My study of corporate law during that year was applied to *The Cooperative Game Theory of the Firm* published by Oxford University Press in 1984.

M. Aoki, *Transboundary Game of Life*,
https://doi.org/10.1007/978-981-13-2757-5_22

Fig. 22.1 Winter in Cambridge, with my family

With me for this year at Harvard was my family, including my daughters who were almost three years old and seven months old. We put our older daughter into a nursery school right off. When the school called to say she wouldn't stop crying, my wife rushed over. As she learned to mimic English as if learning how to sing a song, she eventually began to speak. It must have been hard for our daughters to go along with us to an entirely different place. Our family often went for drives to places like Crane Beach, north of Boston, where we took walks on the beach. I liked the New England seaside with hardly anyone around and nothing but nature as it reminded me of the Shōnan seashore of my childhood (Fig. 22.1).

Returning to Kyoto after this fulfilling year at Harvard, I was able to engage in the kinds of intellectual stimulation unique to Kyoto. One of these was a study group presided over by the late Professor Norio Fujisawa, a scholar of great erudition about Greek philosophy, for whom the adjective "dandy" seemed to fit perfectly. The regulars in the group included scholars in a wide range of fields, such as the late Professor Hayao Kawai (psychology, education).[1] Once a month we would hold discussions while eating a Kyoto-style box dinner; and to finish up we would go to a bar where we were regulars and have a couple of drinks. Professor Kawai was the Chair of the Faculty of Education at Kyoto University, and at times he rushed to our

[1]The late Professor Hayao Kawai has written about this study group in "Geppō" ("Monthly Bulletin") of *Fujisawa Norio chosaku shū* (Collected Works of Norio Fujiwawa), Iwanami Shoten (2000).

gathering from collective bargaining sessions with activists in the student movement. Although he was a tough negotiator against the radical students, his creed was never to negotiate from a position of being above the students. This attitude of his allowed a tacit trust to be built with the radical students. The students accommodated Professor Kawai's clinic hours by releasing him from the collective bargaining sessions when time was up.

I don't recall that we had an official name for this study group, but it was something like "value system for a flourishing society," so we called it "Value Study" ("kachiken"). It lasted about three years. The study group was actually proposed by the Ministry of International Trade and Industry (MITI), but the person in charge insisted on being in the background to allow for a wealth of opinions to be offered. Years later, from among the members of this "Value Study" group, Norio Fujisawa and Hisayasu Nakagawa took posts at the Ministry of Education (Kyoto National Museum Director); Hayao Kawai at the Agency for Cultural Affairs (Commissioner for Cultural Affairs); Kōji Satō became the voice for legal reform (Judicial Reform Council Chairman); and I helped in policy research for economic systems reform (RIETI, Research Institute of International Trade and Industry, Chief Research Officer). This may prove that bureaucrats in the central government had the foresight to consider that a study group like this, which at first glance may not seem to be productive, may be useful in the future.

The reason this study group has such strong memories for me is that Professor Kawai had published his well-received volume *Depth of Japan's Hollow Center Structure* (Chūkō Sōsho), and the discussions in the study group were vividly influenced by his thoughts. By now this concept has become well-known. The hollow center, as Professor Kawai concluded from analyzing the mythology in the *Kojiki* (Record of Ancient Matters), is a deep psychological structure shared by Japanese. In order to keep the equilibrium between the maternal principle and the paternal principle, a non-proactive and non-functional presence is placed between them. (In the *Kojiki*, this would be Tsukuyomi, god of the moon, in the middle between Amaterasu, sun goddess, and her brother Susanoo, god of storms.) This is in contrast to the Western structure of a monolithic principle, which consolidates a system based on a single factor such as power.

It so happened that I had written in my book on corporate governance while at Harvard an idea similar to Professor Kawai's analysis of myths. In the Anglo-American style of firms based on the monolithic principle stocks are the authority (profit maximization) under which the business executive unifies and manages the employees. This format is accomplished by what Professor Kawai calls the paternal principle (hierarchy). However, at that time in Japan business executives functioned to keep the equilibrium between the interests of the firm and the interests of the investors (including the banks). This format wasn't the hollow center structure per se, but the role of the business executive, rather than being proactive, placed importance on harmony within the organization. In that sense it is possible to see it being analogous to the hollow center of mythology presented by Kawai. Similarly, the role of the bureaucracy in Japan's political economic system has an aspect of keeping harmony among various interest groups. There is an aspect in this system that cannot be understood as the implementation of a unilateral paternal principle by the bureaucracy. I discovered that we share a common understanding of the issues in modern Japanese social structure that goes beyond the distinct fields of the humanities and social sciences.

As I mentioned, some twenty years later, Professor Kawai and I worked for the central government and lived in the same civil servant housing area in Sanban-chō, Tokyo. Professor Kawai put his punning wit to use, saying every day was one of thanks ("kansha") and government housing ("kansha"), as those words are homonyms. With his flute, he joined my wife who plays cello and his daughter who worked at the Agency for Cultural Affairs in morning practice of flute trios in our living room, and held some concerts. We moved away before he did; and, feeling nostalgic for the pleasant times we shared, he sent us a postcard saying, "Unfortunately, I've picked up the 'Can't quit the Cultural Agency sickness'." About six months later, he went around to apologize to the local people about the Agency for Cultural Affairs' mismanagement of the conservation of the ancient Takamatsuzuka tomb archaeological site. That evening, he collapsed from a stroke, and several months later passed away without regaining consciousness. When I read Professor Kawai's personal essay collection about his childhood, *Hā-chan the Crybaby* (posthumous publication, Shinchōsha), I can't help but agree with what his widow wrote, that he had already "felt an unknowable fate" awaited him. I think there is something deeper than his having given his life to the mishandling by his organization. It may have been that within Professor Kawai's heart was the heavy feeling of being an "accomplice" regarding the moral hazard we share living in these times, which became evident in the mishandling of the protection of our public asset and in sadness for the ancient builders of the Takamatsuzuka tomb.

Another valuable learning experience I gained at Kyoto University was the importance of fieldwork that I learned from Professors Kazuo Koike and the late Banri Asanuma. When I was visiting at Harvard, and my interest was leaning toward corporate system analysis, I felt like I had been woken up when I came across Professor Koike's *Labor Organizations and Participation in the Workplace* (Tōyō Keizai Shinpōsha).

My work was in mathematical economics, a field unrelated to the workplace. For my research aim of looking at economies from the perspective of information systems, the detailed work of Professor Koike on the mechanism of how knowledge is shared in Japan's factory workplace gave me a micro-micro (meso) foundation. When I returned from America, I was able to persuade my colleagues to invite Professor Koike to Kyoto University's Institute of Economic Studies from Nagoya University. Going to observe factories with him, I learned his fieldwork knowhow and I had much to learn from his attitude toward research that always threw doubts, rich with his sharp observations, upon the meaning of theory and common knowledge.

As Professor Asanuma was an activist in the Bund during the anti-Security Treaty days, it was no coincidence that I shared his interest in Hurwicz-style economic mechanism theory, even before I had taken up my position at Kyoto University. Professor Asanuma came to apply this theoretical grounding to his analysis of factory and management workplace observations, and, conversely, he worked to give feedback to his theory from the knowledge gained in the field. His work made a major impact on the corporate organization theory of Paul Milgrom, John Roberts, and others' comparative system analysis in the early 1990s. A perfectionist who was the model of a sober and honest man, he passed away before he could write up and publish his findings. After his death, through the efforts of Tatsuya Kikutani, whom we both taught and an excellent research assistant to Professor Asanuma, his work was able to be published. This is a brilliant accomplishment on Japan's corporate organization analysis.[2]

Stimulated by such research, I began to sense the need for the publication of an accurate economic analysis of the characteristics of Japanese corporations. This was at a time when the old stereotypes on Japanese economics were still circulating around the world. Gathering colleagues with similar aspirations to analyze the various facets of Japanese corporations, such as work organization on the shop floor, management organization, compensation system, corporate groups, and finance, I formed a study group lasting two years. From Japan, the participants were young scholars beginning to make a mark in international academic circles: the late Tsuneo Ishikawa, Masahiro Okuno, Kazuo Ueda, Toshiaki Tachibanaki, Iwao Nakatani, and Taizō Yakushiji. From abroad, we requested participation in discussions from Mervyn King (now Governor of the Bank of England), the late Harvey Leibenstein (Harvard University), Richard Freeman (Harvard University), and Eleanor Hadley. The resulting volume was published in English as *The Economic Analysis of the Japanese Firm* (North-Holland) in 1984; there is no Japanese translation. I learned that Professor Ronald Dore, perhaps the leading international sociologist on Japan, read this book and recommended it as persuasive, rare for a volume on economics. I was able to avail myself of the opportunity to work together with Professor Dore a decade later and begin an association that continues to this day.[3]

In July 1982, after the final meeting of this project at a hotel in Rokkō, Kobe, the next morning when I went to sign my receipt after breakfast, I was unable to do so. When I tried to write, I couldn't control my index finger. I was suddenly beset with writer's cramp. I had been working on completing the manuscripts for two volumes at the same time. My fingers were affected by the forceful vibrations of the IBM electric typewriter that I had been banging on from morning to night. Those were the days when you had to retype from the start of the page if you made a mistake or changed your mind about what to write.

Since that day, despite undergoing various treatments, I have been unable to write with a pen, and have had to shift to my left hand to sign checks. Having to write left-handed to take notes on my reading and at seminars is quite a handicap for my scholarly work. With the development of word processors and soft-key laptops, I can manage to write my articles. But becoming removed from the act of expression

---

[2] Asanuma, Banri (author) and Tatsuya Kikutani (ed.), *Nihon no kigyō soshiki: kakushinteki tekiō no mekanizumu* (Organization of Japanese firms: mechanism for innovative adaption), Tōyōkeizai Shinpōsha (1998).

[3] Aoki, Masahiko and Ronald Dore (eds.), *The Japanese Firm: Sources of Competitive Strength*, Oxford University Press, 1994.

through what the calligrapher Kyūyō Ishikawa terms the "feel of the brush," I am sure I have lost something. For the title of this series of my memoir, I felt determined to write with a soft brush with my right hand. I hope the reader will excuse my ungainly calligraphy. I hope to devote myself to improving my brush strokes.

Chapter 23
Return to My Former Haunts

My year at Harvard University gave me the impetus to participate in international academic activities, and my exchanges at Kyoto University with scholars in different fields were enjoyable and productive. However, the Institute of Economic Research lost its reformist leaders, such as the late Tsunehiko Watabe; and the problems of a non-academic nature that I faced regarding the post of professor sent me into the doldrums. I came to think my writer's cramp wasn't due merely to a mechanical cause like too much typing.

As I was in this state of mind, I received an invitation to a post at my former place of work, Stanford University. A new chaired professorship on Japanese studies had been set up with the donation of a Japanese Nisei couple named Takahashi, who were business people. Word had been circulating in academic circles that a search was in progress to find a scholar who was in the frontiers of economics, rather than in traditional Japanese studies fields, in view of the economically challenging times. Unexpectedly, this opportunity was presented to me. Apparently, Professors Arrow and Takeshi Amemiya had recommended me to the search committee. When I thought about my children's education and the harshness of urban America, it made me waver, but my wife's words, "Let's go," encouraged me to accept the offer. In the end, this was a good choice for both our children and us.

In March 1984, I went to say my farewell to Kentarō Karōji, who was being treated at the National Cancer Center Hospital in Tokyo. He could no longer open his eyes, but told me, "Is your wife going with you? Go do a good job. I'll do my best, too." Two days later, this guileless and delicate man met his early death. I gave his eulogy at the Aoyama funeral hall, where over 1000 people attended his funeral. The next day I departed for San Francisco.

After he left the world of political activism, Karōji worked in many areas, finally becoming a fisherman in distant-water fisheries. When he returned from the sea, he would go to his wife's family home in Kyoto, his fishing boots still on, and we would enjoy drinking together. He looked refreshed, which suited him well. As some of my ancestors were sailors, we may have shared some of the traits of seamen. Drinking

M. Aoki, *Transboundary Game of Life*,
https://doi.org/10.1007/978-981-13-2757-5_23

Fig. 23.1 Former Chair of Zengakuren Kentarō Karōji with author's daughters (c. 1981)

with him was always enjoyable, and with his final departure, I lost my best drinking buddy. Since then, I have distanced myself from the drinking culture (Fig. 23.1).

It had been sixteen years since I had been at Stanford. At the welcome party given by the university president at his official residence, I talked to a young woman political science professor who had also just arrived, who said her doctoral thesis was on the origins of the Soviet Red Army. The organizer of the Red Army was Trotsky. As I had read Trotsky's book and translated it as a student, we had a lively conversation. Her name was Condoleezza Rice, and she became Secretary of State; she seems a bit too involved in war games now. Under normal circumstances, she is a very decent person.

In California, I was surrounded by bright blue skies and vivid sunsets; students who looked relaxed but were like ducks paddling like crazy beneath the water's surface in competition; and brilliant colleagues. Blessed by this environment, I regained my stamina and became academically productive. After all, that was the time when opinion polls came out with the result that Japan was surpassing the Soviet Union as the number one threat to the U.S. The flip side of this was that interest in knowing about Japan was reaching its height. The undergraduate course on Japanese economics swelled to 180 students, the largest number for an elective course. Among the students were a basketball star, a chess master, the captain of the debate club, and an Olympic medalist in women's swimming. Taking after Professor Koike, I took interested students to tour the assembly plant of the recently established Toyota-GM joint venture on the other side of San Francisco Bay and the laser equipment factory at Hewlett Packard, located across the street from my house.

The custom in America is for students to applaud the professor after the last lecture of the term. This gave me great satisfaction that my efforts were rewarded. There is also a system of students filling in an evaluation form for the course; and they write in their candid comments. For the university, students are valued customers. Comments like "hard to understand because of the professor's accent" I could bear. But I would cock my head in wonder at what the student intended with comments like "the course content is good, but not the professor's clothing style."

At the graduate school level, I offered a new course, "The Modern Firm in Theory and Practice." When I took a leave a few years later and returned to Japan, Professor Paul Milgrom took over this course for me. The notes for this course formed the basis for *Economics, Organization and Management* (Prentice Hall, 1992) that he co-authored with Professor John Roberts.

Putting my course content into theoretical form, in 1988 I published *Information, Incentives, and Bargaining in the Japanese Economy* (Cambridge University Press). This volume was translated into Japanese, Chinese, French, Russian, Spanish, and Italian, and received several international awards as well as the Japan Academy Prize. When I was given an award from Italy, I was interviewed on television. A Stanford University graduate student who was supposedly familiar with my ideas interpreted for me. He was stuck on a question that the Italian announcer had asked. To me, it sounded like "Karōshi." I couldn't imagine that the question was about my old comrade Karōji, but I suddenly guessed it was "karōshi," death from overwork. In Europe, at that time the common awareness was that Japan's international competitiveness was founded on the exploitation of subcontractors and workers. On this point, the understanding in the U.S. was a bit more developed.

In that book, I came up with a comparative mathematical model, "J firm vs. A firm," with the aim of explaining the competitive difference between Japanese and American firms. My model showed that neither type was absolutely superior, and that competitiveness would differ depending on technology and market conditions. There have been some people who, without giving this book a careful read, criticize it as presenting the superiority of the Japanese economy without any critical reflection. But that is not the case at all. I did not align myself with the "Japan as number one" type of thinking popular at that in Japan, taking from Professor Ezra Vogel's book title.

Around this time, in order to realize the plan to open Stanford University's study abroad program in Japan, opportunities for me to negotiate with Japanese government agencies increased. These included the Ministry of Education, Ministry of Finance, Ministry of International Trade and Industry, Ministry of Foreign Affairs; industry associations; and corporations. This "fieldwork" deepened my understanding of the system of coexistence between government agencies and related industry organizations intermediated by "zoku politicians," interest group politicians. I termed this system "bureau pluralism" (put simply, compartmentalized pluralism), meaning that the adjustment of vested interests among interest groups is intermediated by government bureaucracy.

This system that transfers and equalizes the economic rent attained by the competitiveness and protection of export industries to industries and interest groups that lack competitiveness is indeed conducive to equalization. However, as international competition intensifies, it falls into the dilemma of the likelihood of weakening the international competitiveness of export industries. I posited that failure in handling this problem would "bring about apathy and jeopardize efficiency, fairness, political stability, and international harmony." This was at a time when Japan was heading into the economic bubble era, and the media and pundits were in a manic phase, saying "We have nothing more to learn from America."

Unfortunately, in the following decade of the 1990s, my concern materialized. Then, the atmosphere of the media and pundits made a 180° turn, into the extreme depressive state of "the lost decade."[1]

Along with my personal work, in 1987 I was involved in founding the first peer-reviewed, English-language Japanese journal, *Journal of the Japanese and International Economies* (JJIE), and became its first editor-in-chief.[2] The hope was to internationalize Japanese economic research. Top rate researchers from Japan and abroad cooperated in editing the journal. This was my second "intellectual venture." After I served as editor-in-chief for ten years, Takatoshi Itō and Takeo Hoshi took it over, and this year is its twentieth anniversary year. Of the "intellectual ventures" I have participated in starting, this one continues to be the most successful, no doubt due to the management abilities of my two successors. In cooperation with two top-flight research institutes, U.S. National Bureau of Economic Research (NBER) and European Centre for Economic Policy Research (CEPR), JJIE has held regular annual conferences which have become a significant venue for the presentation and discussion of the most recent research on international and Japanese economies.

[1]For my critique of this sort of collective manic depressive phenomenon, refer to my *Utsuriyuku kono jūnen: ugokanu shiten* (Unwavering Coordinates in a Decade of Flux), Nikkei Bijinesujin Bunko, 2002.

[2]*Journal of the Japanese and International Economies*. It was originally published by Academic Press and subsequently acquired by Elsevier.

Chapter 24
Taking Stanford to Japan

In 1991, a student carrying a riding saddle came to my office at Stanford University to seek some advice. She told me her parents were Japanese, but she was born and raised in Costa Rica. Having just returned from two years in Japan with my family, my older daughter was struggling to catch up with science class in middle school; she was also taking horseback-riding lessons at the university stables. I asked this student if she could tutor my daughter, and she replied yes.

As her graduation neared, the student, Akiko Yamazaki, said she wanted to go to Japan, where she had never been. I asked Ken'ichi Imai, the Chair of the Board of Trustees of the Stanford Japan Center (SJC), which had recently opened, if there was some work she could do, and he arranged for her to work as his assistant.

At SJC, Akiko met Jerry Yang and David Filo who were students there at the same time she worked there. I heard that they loved pork cutlet rice bowls, and would save up their transportation costs to afford to eat them. Later, Akiko married Jerry Yang, and now they donate millions of dollars for undergraduate education at Stanford. This is possible because Jerry Yang and David Filo founded the internet company Yahoo!.

Yahoo! was a business venture for them, but participating in founding SJC, where they studied in Kyoto, was my third "intellectual venture." Stanford had study abroad programs in Oxford, Paris, Florence, Berlin, and Moscow where some ten percent of Stanford students went to study for about a year. There was not yet a campus in Asia. In the mid-1980s there was heightened American interest in Japanese technology, and the sentiment to place a campus in Japan grew. With Stanford's know-how about study abroad education programs, a dozen universities such as Harvard, Yale, and Princeton were forming a consortium for Japanese studies and wanted Stanford to operate the program. A colleague said, "Masa, why don't you do it?" And, being imprudent, I ended up taking this on.

This turned out to be a much larger job than I had anticipated. Within Stanford, the practice was for each internal venture to gather its own funds, while the Japanese studies professors in the consortium's ten universities were not versed in fund-raising. Furthermore, establishing a campus in Japan by an American university was unprece-

M. Aoki, *Transboundary Game of Life*,
https://doi.org/10.1007/978-981-13-2757-5_24

Fig. 24.1 At the construction site for Stanford Japan Center

dented at that time, which aroused wariness from the Ministry of Education with its fear that a hole might be made in its solid wall of university management. At that time I also held a post as faculty at Kyoto University, and as a member of the international exchange committee I knew that Kyoto University President Yasunori Nishijima, who had studied abroad as an early Fulbright scholar, was very enthusiastic about educational and academic international exchange. But it was out of the question that such a program would be housed and exchanges between Japanese and American students would be encouraged on the Kyoto University campus, as it was a national asset. And yet, in 2005, when the Stanford overseas program opened in China, it was located squarely on the Peking University campus.

In order to realize SJC and the ten-university consortium, it was necessary to secure a building, comply with numerous regulations, and, most urgent of all, raise funds for this venture. I returned to Kyoto and threw myself into this project for two years. I went around to nearly one hundred leading Japanese companies, and with a batting average of 0.980, gathered some $8 million in donations, and received $1 million in funds from Kyoto City, to open SJC in the fall of 1989. I was greatly supported in the fund-raising efforts by former Kyoto University President Michio Okamoto, President Yasunori Nishijima, and the late Osamu Uno, President of the Kansai Economic Federation. Being in the midst of the economic bubble era, companies were willing to make donations. Among industrial and university circles there was eagerness to return the favor that Japan had received from the U.S. during the postwar recovery through Fulbright funds and other American educational subsidies. Government officials in the Ministry of Finance, Ministry of Foreign Affairs, and Ministry of International Trade and Industry who had studied abroad were supportive as well. Everyone was still looking outwardly, showing that not all of the effects of the economic bubble were negative (Fig. 24.1).

The opening ceremony was an illustrious affair attended by the Stanford University president, several deans and department chairs, and some twenty of the first enrolled students as we hosted the Japan's Crown Prince and U.S. Ambassador Michael Armacost. The Center's building was located on leased land in a quiet district near Nanzenji temple, with the spectacular backdrop of Higashiyama, the eastern hills. Allow me to quote from the somewhat sentimental words I wrote as my personal involvement in this intellectual venture came to a close.

> Along with my wife and two daughters who were able to join me in attending the opening reception, I walked home on the Philosophers' Walk amid the tourists viewing the later than usual fall foliage. What drifted into my mind was a personal sense of contentment that in the future my daughters might comprehend the meaning of what—in throwing myself into this work for the past few years, hardly spending any time with my family—their father had accomplished by leaving something in this world. Stanford Japan Center, which for me felt as if I were sending out my daughter in marriage, will become independent. By taking one foot out of this project, it was time for me to return to my long-awaited main work within the academic world.

The funny thing about America is that when I returned to Stanford, the dean sent me a letter noting that my annual salary would increase as a reward for the work I had done to establish SJC. This salary increase would directly affect my pension on retirement, meaning that this intellectual venture of mine was not only beneficial for my own emotional well-being, but also unexpectedly positive for my personal financial status.

Since its founding, SJC has been led in turn by Thomas Rohlen, Ken'ichi Imai, Shin Yasunobe, and Toshihiko Hayashi, who served as directors; by Terry MacDougall, directing the educational program; and staff members. Through their efforts, there have been notable results in research and education. The Kyoto Consortium for Japanese Studies (KCJS: expanded to fourteen participating universities) has educated over 750 students; and the Stanford Center for Technology and Innovation (SCTI) program for engineering students has educated over 550 students since the start of SJC. Among them are Jerry Yang, the founder of Yahoo, and his cohorts; and David Greenspan, a Harvard University economics major, who received the award for best short film at the Cannes International Film Festival with his film "Bean Cake" ("Ohagi"); and a female diplomat who became in charge of the Japan desk at the State Department. I am sure that those who studied at SJC will become ever more active in various fields.

As for research, there have been unique achievements in areas of the social impact of IT (information technology). Gradually it appeared that there was a distance between the initial ideal of being a place for joint research between Japan and the U.S. and the reality that developed. This was the result of the tendency of actual research being conducted independently by Stanford researchers and Japanese corporations, as the overestimation about Japanese technology during the economic bubble period later subsided. It can also be said it was due to the maturation of Stanford's international joint research know-how. Moreover, at Stanford the interest gained on its endowment exceeded 20% at times, but with Japan's low interest rate, it was difficult to maintain the Center's building. This situation ended up causing much hardship for Professor Ken'ichi Imai and others who administered SJC.

Fortunately, Japanese national universities are changing under the system of independent administrative institutions, allowing them more autonomy to follow new directions. With this development, in an effort to deepen the exchanges between

American and Japanese students, SJC cancelled its contract for its own building in 2006, and moved KCJS to the Kyoto University campus and SJC to the Doshisha University campus.[1] Despite the fear of experts that Japanese studies are in decline in the U.S., these programs continue to be popular among American students. Popular culture expressed through manga and anime attract students. At Stanford, there are ideas to expand the SCTI programs from engineering students to wider fields of study.

In the research area, there are new possibilities for international academic and intellectual exchanges being considered with the participation of former Ambassador Armacost, who was at the opening ceremony and is now a fellow at Stanford's Asia-Pacific Research Center, to replace the model of joint industry-academic research put forth fifteen years ago. One such idea is a Stanford Kyoto Pan-Asian forum to discuss mutual items of interest, such as the environment, the aging population, and security issues among Japan, China, and South Korea with the cooperation of Kyoto City.

These developments are what could be called a restructuring of the intellectual venture born in the era of the economic bubble. Restructuring is not a negative countermeasure of what is generally accepted in Japan as a down-scaling and employment adjustment; rather it is a reformist adaptation to the problems presented by a new age through aggressive intentions and ideas.

[1] Translator's Note: Both programs are now on the Doshisha University campus.

Chapter 25
Toward a Comparative Institutional Analysis

The northern California town of Mendocino, which was the shooting background for the film "East of Eden" starring James Dean, retains some of the air of its late nineteenth century role as a harbor to ship out lumber cut from the mountainsides. Ex-hippies-turned-farmers and artists live in the surrounding area. In the latter half of the 1990s, we rented a house facing the Pacific Ocean from an artist every summer. My wife and daughters went back and forth to Stanford for their activities, but I burrowed myself there for the summer with our dog Robin, brought back with us from Japan, and focused on writing my survey on comparative institutional analysis: *Toward a Comparative Institutional Analysis* (MIT Press, 2001). Mornings and evenings I took Robin for a walk on the cape where there was a greater than 180° view. In the morning, the horizon was veiled in fog, while in the evening the ocean was tinted red by the setting sun. It was the perfect place for rethinking problems and reorganizing chapters. Robin was a small mixed breed with some Shikoku-ken, but she was stubborn and at times got into fights with a large Coast Guard officer's watch dog. My family enjoyed meals made from the organic produce we bought at the farmers' market (so many varieties of tomatoes); we also went to the harbor to buy albacore tuna and fresh sea urchin still in its thorny shell.

I began my work on comparative institutional analysis in earnest in 1990. That was the year we began offering a doctorate in the field of comparative institutional analysis (taking its initials: CIA) at Stanford University's Economics Department at the graduate level. This was my fourth "intellectual venture" (Fig. 25.1).

There are diverse forms of market economies due to differences in corporate organizations, legal regulations, and societal norms. There are also diversities in nations (forms of statehood) as studied by political science. CIA attempts to understand the interrelationships among these institutions using the language of game theory. With the dissolution of the Soviet bloc there is no longer relevance in the outmoded comparative economic systems theory of "capitalism versus socialism." But that does not mean that the world's economies all smoothly shift to becoming market economies as assumed by neo-classical economics. In my research into the comparative systems of Japanese and American economies, I found that there were differences that could

M. Aoki, *Transboundary Game of Life*,
https://doi.org/10.1007/978-981-13-2757-5_25

Fig. 25.1 Lecturing on "CIA"

not be explained away by stating that the forms might differ at first glance, but the functions are the same. Isn't a coherent system made up from the interrelationship among society, politics, and economics? How will these differences in characteristics adapt as the market becomes ever more globalized? I wanted to think about such issues by going beyond a mere comparison between the U.S. and Japan. In order to accomplish this, I felt it was necessary to go beyond the limitations of one individual by engaging in discussions with colleagues who held similar approaches to these issues. In terms of my own history, I wanted to find a path to approach the issue of a unified social science that I had left unresolved from the 1970s.

First-rate scholars gathered to study the field of CIA.[1] Paul Milgrom is well-known even in Japan for his text on the theory of organizations and for designing the auction system for radio frequency licenses. The theory that he was working on, which he explained to me by scribbling formulae on the back of a paper napkin at a cafe after a seminar, later became an indispensable analytical tool for analyzing the institutional complementarity of various systems. Assistant professors who participated were: Avner Greif, Yingyi Qian, Marcel Fafchamps, and John Litvack. Greif was the first to tie game theory to critical analysis of historical documents, and had made major achievements in comparative historical research of medieval trade. As a favored student of Professors Janos Kornai and Eric Maskin at Harvard University, Qian made innovative contributions to research on Sino-Soviet comparative systems in the shift from planned economies to market economies. He had a leadership role among graduate students in economics sent from post-Cultural Revolution China. With his wealth of fieldwork on African economies as his background, Fafchamps came up with unique results regarding the roles of trust and reputation in the development of market economies. From before the dissolution of the Soviet Union, Litvack

[1] A major source of understanding and support for launching this unique research project was then NTT Data President Shirō Fujita. There may have been the financial capacity to fund such initiatives by Japanese firms of that time, but I was grateful for the contribution to the academic field by this firm to the experimental and leading edge CIA project. I note my appreciation here.

had done cutting edge work on using game theory to analyze the problem areas of the mechanism of planned economies. I joined them by bringing my comparative U.S.–Japan analytical model.

As noted above, comparative institutional analysis attempts to understand, as an integrated whole, various systems such as markets, societal norms, and nation states. The concept of "equilibrium" among the interactions of the various social games plays an important role. However, as games can have many equilibria, game theory alone cannot offer a self-contained explanation of why and how diverse systems come about. It is essential that differences in systems be described and comparative and historical information on various systems and game theory analysis be integrated in order to understand how different systems arose from their historical backgrounds, what kinds of performance differences come about as a result, and whether they can be maintained as markets globalize. With these points in mind, our field of CIA was launched with this well-rounded and talented membership. Our international reputation was high as well.

Stanford was teeming with prominent scholars interested in institutional analysis in fields other than economics: Mark Granovetter, James March, and Walter Powell in Sociology; Barry R. Weingast and Stephen D. Krasner in Political Science; John Roberts and John McMillan of Business and Economics. Called "the Farm" from its inception due to its previous use, a rural atmosphere remained on the Stanford campus, with many of the faculty and students living on or near the campus. This offered an ideal environment for close social interaction and tangible and intangible exchanges that went beyond particular academic disciplines.

Drawn by the appeal of this atmosphere, Douglass North came each winter from Washington University in St. Louis and often participated in our seminars. In the summer of 1993, I was invited along with him to the meeting of the Royal Swedish Academy of Engineering Sciences; and we went to the opera under the midnight sun. He said, "This is so much fun, let's come again." And, he actually did go to Stockholm at the end of that year to receive the Nobel Prize in Economics. This was a great encouragement to those of us in institutional analysis research.

In writing *Toward a Comparative Institutional Analysis*, my stays at the Swedish Collegium for Advanced Studies in Social Sciences, the London School of Economics, and the Max Planck Institute for the Study of Societies were helpful. Also unforgettable were the three months I lectured at University of Tokyo in the fall of 1994, invited by Professor Masahiro Okuno and Associate Professor Tetsuji Okazaki. Other than the lectures, my time was spent cooped up in my room in the University's dormitory for foreign researchers in Shirogane, Tokyo, writing up my lecture notes. The building was so drab that I thought, "My cell at Sugamo prison was better than this." There was a pink pay telephone for international calls in the room. Based on my lecture notes, I published "The evolution and diversity of economic systems" (Toyo Keizai Shinpōsha: 1995). I didn't think it would take long to turn this into an English version, but it took five years to complete it to my satisfaction. Finally, in 2001, it was simultaneously published in Japanese, English and Chinese (the French translation came in 2007), under the English title *Information, Corporate Governance and Institutional Diversity* (Oxford University Press: 2000). The draft of this work allowed me to receive the Joseph Schumpeter Prize from the International Joseph A. Schumpeter Society in 1998 at the Shönbrunn Palace in Vienna.

But, unsurprisingly, all was not smooth sailing in my life. April 1, 1998 turned out to be the worst birthday in my life. That day, the Economics Department at Stanford University held a faculty meeting to discuss whether Yingyi Qian should be promoted from assistant professor to a tenured position. In the decade preceding this time, the Economics Department had granted this promotion to only a few scholars, and this high threshold was well-known within American academia. Qian had published articles in rapid succession in highly regarded academic journals, and some dozen selected scholars in the front lines of research in theoretical economics and institutional analysis from around the world all recommended his promotion. Despite this, the decision to grant him a tenured position was vetoed by a few hard-liners.

As it is against the code of ethics of American universities to divulge the content of such meetings regarding hiring, I cannot discuss this matter. But in fact, there were people outside the proceedings who suspected that the opposition was based on non-scholarly emotions against this international field, which was overwhelmingly popular among foreign students. In any event, it cannot be denied that this outcome was a setback for the research organization of comparative institutional analysis at Stanford University. It was also a major blow to me as a fellow Asian colleague as we had encouraged each other.

This episode is an example of the cutthroat competition in American academia for the expansion of influence of research methods within various fields. In order to survive in those circumstances, one must have tenacious willpower and staying power so as not to be defeated by those pressures. As for Yingyi Qian, he became a professor at University of California, Berkeley, and in 2006 became the fourth Dean of the School of Economics and Management at Tsinghua University in China. The founding Dean was Zhu Rongji, who for several years held the post concurrently while he was the Chinese Premier. Fafchamps became director of the Centre for the Study of African Economies at Oxford University; and Litvak became an economist at the World Bank.

As a result of this situation, and as I had moved my base of operations to Japan for a while, the field of CIA, after some ten years of activity, discontinued its formal structure, and is now being continued on a more compact scale by Greif. Within the large market of economics, this "venture" created a niche market, but perhaps this was insufficient to make it an influential enterprise. Or, perhaps it was at the stage of spinning off other ventures throughout the world. In any case, venture start-ups face ups and downs. My strong feeling is that the spirit and ideas of this venture, unlike the case of the Bund, has not completed its role, and will continue to live on. I can only agree with the philosopher J. R. Searle of University of California, Berkeley, that "Given the centrality of institutional phenomena, it is somewhat surprising that institutional economics has not always been at the center of mainstream economics".[2]

[2]Searle, John R. "What is an Institution?" *Journal of Institutional Economics*, Vol. 1 (1), (2005), p. 2.

Chapter 26
To Kasumigaseki

In July 1997, I was allotted a corner office on the second floor of the Ministry of International Trade and Industry's main building in Kasumigaseki, Tokyo. I was eating lunch in my new office with Osamu Watanabe, the administrative vice minister. He welcomed me as the Director of the Research Institute of Economy, Trade and Industry, succeeding Professor Ryūtarō Komiya (Fig. 26.1).

I couldn't help saying, "Exactly below this window is where things started for me." The Kasumigaseki intersection, hemmed in by the Ministry of Foreign Affairs, Ministry of Finance, Ministry of Agriculture and Fisheries, and Ministry of International Trade and Industry was the very spot where, in November 1959, Saburō Eda, organizing bureau head of the Japan Socialist Party, with a diagonal sash across his chest, called out, "To the Diet!" and led the demonstration from this spot. Inexplicably, that demonstration actually entered the Diet Building grounds, starting off the anti-Security Treaty political season.

Trading places: Economist takes helm of government agency in Japan

BY KATHLEEN O'TOOLE

When Japan was dominated by a shogun military commander, he required feudal lords to alternate residence between their castle towns and Edo, now Tokyo. Masa Aoki, the Takahashi Professor of Economics at Stanford, likes to joke that he is returning to that lifestyle.

Last July, Japan's powerful Ministry of International Trade and Industry – MITI for short – announced that it was tapping the 59-year-old economist to head its research institute. As a result, Aoki will alternate his residence between Stanford and Tokyo, although he spent last quarter in a third locale – the London School of Economics. In the shogun era, alternating residences was a system for controlling the shogun's potential rivals, Aoki says, but it also enhanced communication by spreading knowledge of local craft and industrial practices, precisely what Aoki aims to do.

At his first press conference as MITI research director last summer, Aoki said Japan's corporate structure "is getting too fat" and must slim down to head off long-term stagnation of the Japanese economy. Based on a recommendation he made several years ago, the government enacted a law permitting holding companies for the

'People in Europe lump the problems of Japan, Thailand and Korea together as an East Asian crisis, but the problems are very different in each country' Aoki said.

ECONOMICS PROFESSOR MASA AOKI juggles the demands of academic life here and his responsibilities as head of a government research agency in Tokyo.

cies are run by insiders. The ministries attract some of the country's brightest college graduates, Aoki said, and then promote some to leadership positions. In this case, Aoki said, he will be more like a chairman of a board than a day-to-day director, so he can continue to teach at

Aoki's reputation is built upon his comparative analyses of Japanese and U.S. industrial structures and on his work for the World Bank on desirable financial systems for transition economies. Government, he says, can play a complementary role to business and enhance markets in

"In the 1950s, Japanese businessmen discovered they had a huge productivity gap with American companies like U.S. Steel and General Motors, so they started to learn American quality control and scientific management methods," he says. "These methods had been designed by engineers and imposed on workers. The Japanese modified it in such a way that quality control was discussed by engineers and workers on the shop floor. In this way, they developed a new type of quality control and a system to reduce costly inventories."

It was a Japanese organizational innovation, but one that resulted from "combining the traditional Japanese cooperative team approach with American scientific management."

Falling behind, American companies then looked at Japanese firms' lean production methods. Instead of controlling inventories within a tightly organized *keiretsu*, or conglomerate, Aoki says, they focused on designing basic products and writing standards for components, which then could be manufactured by others throughout the world. Using advanced technology in communication and transportation, they downsized the firm and developed a more flexible, modular organization.

"Now is the time when the Japanese should learn from us. There is a way for

Fig. 26.1 Stanford Daily reporting on my "trading places"

M. Aoki, *Transboundary Game of Life*,
https://doi.org/10.1007/978-981-13-2757-5_26

It was only natural that I asked myself, "What is the 'wall' that separates me as I stand here now with the street below?" It may very well be that I had pursued the research topic of "What is an institution? How can institutions change?" in order to answer that question in my own personal history. From my amicable discussions with Douglass North, the major force in new institutional studies, rather than "Politics changes institutions" (North), I had come to think that the form of a nation's society and politics mutually influence each other as they change by coevolution. From that perspective going over that "wall" was to go beyond the "internal versus external" fictitious wall. This would allow me to glimpse how Japan might change or if it cannot change, giving me an opportunity to participate in that process from my position as an academic. North had urged me, saying "It will be good fieldwork for institutional research." To be sure, as I will show later, I was faced with not a fictitious wall but a real wall, as I came to deepen my understanding of its characteristics.

As Director of the Research Institute of Economy, Trade and Industry, my position was part-time, so I was expected to go in several times a year. MITI assumed my role would be something like an academic advisor supporting the policy research of officials. The Stanford Daily campus newspaper reported my going to the MITI Research Institute to be "trading places," with an occasional appearance there. But it became clear that my intention of going there occasionally would not last long. At MITI, under Prime Minister Ryūtarō Hashimoto's administration, the ministry was searching for its format under its restructuring as the Ministry of Economy, Trade, and Industry (METI). Among the young reformists were those like Kōji Matsui (now member of House of Councilors) who were ardently working for "leading the reform of Kasumigaseki" by turning the Research Institute into an independent administrative institution. That being the case, I began to think that I would be willing to work with them to form a serious think tank in Japan, along the lines of the operational examples of the well-respected Brookings Institution and the Stanford Institute for Economic Policy Research.

The existing state of research institutes within ministries entailed these conditions: (1) researchers were mainly from the career bureaucrats in within the ministry, with the participation of a few on loan from universities; (2) researchers could make quasi-academic research presentations, but they customarily did not make policy proposals that went against the benefit of the ministry either as individuals or as a team. However, they did administrative work for conference preparations; (3) the director was an academic advisor, the actual management being done by the deputy director who was a career bureaucrat.

However, if we were to create the kind of high-quality policy research think tank not yet existing in Japan, using the advantage of the new system of independent administration institutions, I considered there to be three essential points. (1) The research institution should be formed with research fellows gathered from beyond MITI in a collaboration among "industry, academia, and private" sectors; (2) individual researchers would take initiative and responsibility and focus on their own research while professional support staff would be hired for such tasks as editing, website management, and conference support; (3) the post of chair and director would be split: the director would oversee the personnel matters of researchers by assessing their research, but if the basic direction of the research framework is mistaken, the chair can fire the director. The director's compensation would be an annual salary based on market value, and no retirement fee will be paid.

Even now, I think that these three points are the essential conditions for creating a viable policy research think tank. If the aim becomes to reach a consensus for policy proposals and comply with short-term benefits, and the individual researcher's presence becomes invisible, the researchers' incentives degrade and the quality of the research declines. Furthermore, if the chair who is not a research professional holds sway over personnel matters of researchers, it becomes undesirable in terms of the protection of quality and freedom of research and the prevention of direct political interference. This idea is like that of corporate governance in which the chairman of the board of directors and the CEO are split up, so that the research director has clear authority and responsibility to execute the work in the specialized field.

As soon as I took up my post, I formed an informal committee for the review of the research institute headed by Shin Yasunobe, director of electronic policy division (now president of Future Architect), a leader of the young officials. This committee gathered some fifteen exceptionally bright young MITI officials to discuss what topics are important in policy research. I think these discussions were very useful to all of the participants. About half of the members are now active as directors of front line divisions at METI, and the others include a member of parliament, a university professor, and the president of a leading corporation.

One of the pressing topics the committee took up, with its research result forcefully presented as a policy proposal, was "University Reform: topics and arguments" (*Daigaku kakumei* (University reform), Aoki, Masahiko, Akihiro Sawa, and Michio Daidō, eds. Tōyō Keizai Shinpōsha, 2001). As industry-academia cooperation and the shifting of universities to the oversight of the framework of independent administrative institutions had become important agenda items, fortunately, this volume was widely read. One of the experiments under item (1) above was the participation from a Swiss university in a project by Yūko Harayama (now Professor at Tohoku University), who was researching Stanford's industry-academia collaboration through studying university archives and interviews of deans of the engineering school.

I myself also participated in formulating plans for industry-academia alliances and national university reforms as a member of the Science and Technology Council. Under discussion at that time was how to advance the shift of national universities to become independent administration institutions and how to increase the mobility of researchers between universities. These two issues actually should and could be solved as a unit. One leading politician was so enthusiastic about "reform" that he suggested the latter issue be resolved by law. It was a suggestion to restrict the number of professors who were graduates of the same university to under 40%. I hammered home my point that "even at Cambridge and Harvard, more than 50% of their professors were educated at their respective universities," to finally get him to withdraw this idea that would no doubt have had devastating consequences.

The mobility of faculty at American universities is realized by salaries set at market rates, as in the case of professional baseball players; and the effect of this incentive maintains the high quality of research and teaching. In contrast, many of the problems in Japanese universities derive from the fact that, from an early stage in their careers, researchers' salaries are uniformly set by the civil service grade chart, and thus they are isolated from the competitive challenge of mid-career hires from outside academia.

Although a single effort would not solve all the problems, if the faculty are no longer civil servants, a basic course could be pursued. However, as this direction received major resistance from university faculty, the Ministry of Education could not outwardly shift its cautious stance. Yet there were those within the Ministry of Education who were preparing for this shift. Therefore, this problem was brought to a resolution by the positive administrative guidance of Prime Minister Jun'ichirō Koizumi's administration. The results of this reform are still to come, but it is certain that an air of freedom has become noticeable in Japanese universities since that time.

The enthusiasm for reforms of the time acted as the lubricating oil, and with the support of Minister of State for Economic and Fiscal Policy, Financial Services Kaoru Yosano, Vice Minister Katsusada Hirose, and Director General Hidehiro Konno at MITI, plans to shift the Research Institute to an independent administrative institution were progressing along the lines discussed above. But, as in the phrase "the mummy hunter becomes the mummy," as the time to establish this new setup approached, I was pushed into the position of having to take on the directorship. In this manner, the independent administrative institution Research Institute of Economy, Trade and Industry (RIETI) with me as President and Chief Research Officer (CRO), was launched in April 2001. METI provided excellent management and research personnel, beginning with Executive Vice President Nobuo Tanaka (now Executive Director, International Energy Agency) and Director of Research Akihiro Sawa (now Professor, University of Tokyo). The Ministry also funded the hiring of researchers and staff from the private sector with special capabilities, experience, and expertise. With these felicitations, my fifth intellectual venture was launched.

However, I did not yet realize that stepping over the ingrained customs of Kasumigaseki's administrative institutions would result in incurring dangerous risks.

Chapter 27
Light and Shadow of Independent Administrative Institutions

For two years after the launch of RIETI in 2001, its leadership, researchers, and staff were united in the enthusiasm to create "Kasumigaseki Team II" (Fig. 27.1). I think it was Executive Vice President Nobuo Tanaka who coined that term, intending it to mean that RIETI would engage in long-term policy research which could not be done in the Ministry. He and I were involved in a workshop when he was the Deputy-Director of Science, Technology, and Industry at Organisation for Economic Co-operation and Development (OECD). And, as he had observed the workings of the Brookings Institution and other American think tanks when he was posted as Minister for Energy, Trade and Industry at the Japanese Embassy in Washington, D.C., he was a close colleague of mine. We did not subscribe to the notion of "the lost decade," the depressive view popular at the time, as we aggressively pursued the potential for institutional change. During the three years I was at my post, we put out commercially based publications from Tōyō Keizai Shinpōsha: over ten volumes each on a full-fledged "Economic Policy Analysis Series" (*Fiscal Reforms of Japan: Redesigning the Frame of the State*, Aoki, Masahiko and Kōtarō Tsuru, authors and editors) and policy-oriented "Economic Policy Review Series" (*Modularity: A New Industrial Architecture*, Aoki, Masahiko and Haruhiko Andō, authors and editors). These reached a standard we could be proud of. This work led many to start on the path of becoming first-rate researchers.

There were many other innovative milestones. Borrowing the custom of brown bag lunches common at American universities and research institutes, we invited a wide range of participants from other ministries and the mass media and created a place for casual circulation of information. This format has gained wider presence in Kasumigaseki.

RIETI's website was developed with researchers' columns cultivating fans with great leaps in the number of hits. Access to the website by mass media journalists and private sector researchers became common. When we started a Chinese language section of the website, alongside Japanese and English, Chinese government officials and academics welcomed the fact that they could access discussion on Japanese economic policy directly without going through English. We organized an annual

M. Aoki, *Transboundary Game of Life*,
https://doi.org/10.1007/978-981-13-2757-5_27

Fig. 27.1 As Director of RIETI, lecturing at Keio University (photo courtesy of Bungei Shunjusha)

international symposium, the RIETI Asian Network of Economic Policy Research (ANEPR), to create a means of communication among economists from Asia and the West on important policy topics, such as corporate governance and Asian market integration. The work of the staff to implement these events was a great accomplishment.

Later, in the winter of 2006, there was conflict in the Council on Economy and Fiscal Policy concerning the basic policy between then Minister Kaoru Yosano and Minister of Internal Affairs and Communications Heizō Takenaka.[1] The economic advisors to these two politicians were Kōtarō Tsuru and Yōichi Takahashi, respectively, both of whom had been members of the fiscal reform project at RIETI. As the possibilities for regime change and major coalitions increase in the future, it is essential that we have a shared knowledge base and data as foundations for political discussions and that these discussions be founded on accurate theories and facts. The role of policy think tanks will become more important to prepare for these realities.

By the third year after the launch of this think tank, while on one hand some researchers were recognized by the public for their spectacular research results, on the other hand there were those among the bureaucrats tasked with low-level work in the ministries who became resentful. Assessment of a venture in the marketplace does not pose any problems, but among government bureaucrats who were long-time stagehands, some burned with jealousy toward the successes of their more recognized colleagues. Part of the responsibility for this morass lay in my lack of understanding about the subtlety and stagnation of Japanese organizational culture.

In addition, the problematic aspects of the half measures of the system of "independent administrative institutions" grew evident. Though termed "independent,"

[1] Shimizu (2007).

the management class personnel were incorporated into the personnel rotation system or the practice of placing former bureaucrats in those institutions. These newly assigned people did not always fully understand the initial mission of the independent administrative institution system. It is possible that there were those who thought of this type of atmosphere within government agencies to be "outrageous to have a Kasumigaseki Team II." These people began to strengthen their bureaucratic management in the time-honored way, whether consciously or habitually. Among them were even those who treated fellows and staff recruited from outside the organization in an uncivil manner. As I stated in "Chap. 11: Collapse of the Bund," this situation was unforgivable from my organizational philosophy in which I saw the venture-type organization as a mediating agency for the spontaneity and autonomy of its members.

Another problem was the structure of layer upon layer of overseeing bodies, with each independent administrative institution having an evaluation sub-committee, with an evaluation committee at the ministerial level above it, and an evaluation committee of the Ministry of Internal Affairs above that. It was a natural consequence that even if at the independent administrative institution level the sub-committee worked from their specialist position, the overseeing agency and chair of the board would gradually turn their focus on the non-specialist level above, and start to interfere in specific research structures and research content.[2]

The ideal situation would be a decentralized form of governance by which the chair of the board of each independent administrative institution is accountable to its evaluation sub-committee that has specialized knowledge, and the committee above monitors only the validity of the composition and selection process of each independent administrative institution's evaluation committee. This is a good way to reflect the popular will, filtered through the specialists at the independent administrative institution level, in its activities. Furthermore, in the event of posting career officials from the ministry to the independent administrative institution, there should be a method of guaranteeing their loyalty to the purpose of the independent administrative institution such as a policy of not returning to their ministry for a minimum of five years.

But such a system was not possible other than in an academic's theoretical terms. My three principles for the ideal policy research think tank as stated in "Chap. 26:

---

[2]From what I hear, the oversight evaluation committee recently downgraded RIETI for the reason that the implementation of competitive research funding was lagging. However, it is neither possible nor advisable that a policy research institute like RIETI compete with universities for research funding. This kind of hierarchical governance that issues such an evaluation is so characteristically bureaucratic, and a waste of the efforts to establish the system of "independent administrative institutions." In the mid-1990s there was a similar hierarchical governance "reform" plan suggested for state corporations in China; if that had been selected, today's Chinese economic development would have been inconceivable. Related to the same METI issues, there is currently an initiative under consideration for Nippon Export and Investment Insurance (NEXI) to become a special public corporation; but this way of thinking is off the mark at this time when a national strategy is required for securing of resources. This is for the sake of convenience to accomplish the results of "reform" by merely changing formats of organizations or juggling the numbers. Straying off course in these ways arises from the failure to design a governance structure that can evaluate and monitor each independent administrative institution on its own merits from a public and specialized perspective.

To Kasumigaseki" were gradually whittled away. I felt that my powers did not meet the test for overcoming this resistance under the present rules of the legal system of independent administrative institutions.[3] It appeared that my expectation was too optimistic about the possibility for attitudinal change by bureaucrats on how to play the game. Realizing that there was nothing more that I could do, I submitted my resignation to the board chair after three years into my term, even though two years remained.[4] I considered myself to be taking responsibility by turning on its head the third rule of my three principles ("if the basic direction of the research framework is mistaken, the chair can fire the director"). Many of the fellows and staff left RIETI along with me. Among them were those who had participated from abroad: Ronald Dore, Gerald L. Curtis, and Meng Jianjun.

Some in the major mass media stated this change in RIETI metaphorically as "appearing like a comet, and disappearing like a comet." This fifth venture of mine ended as a half measure, or as a setback. RIETI evaluation sub-committee chair Yoshihiko Miyauchi expressed his disappointment, saying, "If only you could have held on for a while longer." Others advised me in the opposite direction, "Get away as fast as you can from this powder house." In the event, thinking of the academic work that still remained for me, I lacked the capacity for persistence needed to patiently manage the organization toward my ideal while making certain compromises within the framework of the slowly increasing stranglehold of administrative governance. When I left RIETI, the atopic rash that had bothered me toward the end of my time there disappeared as if by magic.

When I recall the three years I spend at RIETI, I still cannot rid myself of the thought that in terms of my own research it might have been a waste of time. But I am also confident that I put all my energy into this venture during that time. Even now I am glad to hear that most of the fellows and staff that worked with me at RIETI look back fondly on the passionate atmosphere and research results, regretting their passing. I do feel regret and am sorry that my powers were insufficient to continue that venture.

Through this experience, I came to a deep understanding that true "reform" (system transformation) is not attainable by mere organizational adjustment, such as forming an "independent administrative institution," but requires a deep connection

---

[3]This type of experiment may require governance by a private foundation, such as the Brookings Institution, or placement under open, public governance by a parliament with near-parity between ruling and opposition parties.

[4]Nobuo Ikeda, who was a Fellow at RIETI during its first three years, has written the following in his blog, which has been quoted by others on the internet. "… Takao Kitahata, then deputy vice minister (now administrative vice minister) … put pressure on Chairman Sōzaburō Okamatsu to replace Director Aoki and expel the "Aoki faction" researchers. As a result, Director Aoki resigned in 2004, and most of the researchers he had invited from elsewhere (including myself) resigned as well. Those Aoki faction researchers who remained were targets of harassment, such as not having their research expenses funded, and most of them resigned." This explanation is overly political and not accurate. I resigned not because of "pressure" from the Ministry, but of my own will due to differences in "views of institutions" and "ideology" about organizations; and I think most of the researchers, other than Mr. Ikeda, felt the same way as I had.

to changing people's mind sets.[5] I also gained results in my fieldwork to improve my understanding of the subtle wrinkles in Japanese organizations: Japanese organizational culture, the relationship between bureaucracy and politics, and the involvement of mass media in politics.

To this day I value the transboundary network assets that I gained among the superior officials seriously working on public issues at Kasumigaseki whom I met during my time there. There are all sorts of criticisms about the way the government operates out of Kasumigaseki, and at times I am filled with righteous indignation. Needless to say, however, there is a role for bureaucracy. It was just not a world in which I could live in comfort.

[5]For this reason, I am using the phrase "Belief-Institution Co-evolution Process" as a specialized term to concisely express the essence of social change. Here "Belief" means the "shared awareness" about the way social games are played. For further reading see: Aoki, Masahiko, "Understanding Douglass North in the Game-Theoretic Language," http://papers.ssrn.com/sol3/papers.cfm?abstract_id=1083790.

Chapter 28
Engaging with China

Recently, whether in Japan or abroad, I am often asked, "Where are you living now?" The answer is that half the time I live in the U.S., a little less than half in Japan, and the other month or so I travel to China or Europe. Having retired from my chaired professorship at Stanford University three years ago, I became a senior fellow at the Institute for International Studies. I am also visiting professor at the Graduate School of International Corporate Strategy at Hitotsubashi University, through the introduction by Professors Hirotaka Takeuchi and Ikujirō Nonaka. From April 2007, responding to the leadership of Chair Hideki Katō, I am participating as distinguished fellow at Tokyo Foundation.

There is no mandatory retirement age for professors in the U.S., but it takes a lot of physical and mental energy to teach undergraduates who are highly demanding. At Stanford, the usual load for undergraduate courses is one hour classes from Monday through Friday, on top of which there are almost weekly quizzes and reports, though, thankfully, these are graded by teaching assistants. This schedule is tough for students, but it is also hard labor for professors who must teach for a full ten weeks per term. In addition, there are graduate school level courses and doctoral thesis advising. As they are deeply related to my own research, there is less of a sense of burden to teach at the graduate level when compared to undergraduate teaching, and more of a sense of satisfaction. Since these graduate students are engaged in stiff competition to become established scholars on their own, it is essential that we professors continue to push ahead with leading edge research or they will not take notice of us.

Taking these factors into account, at my age and experience, I thought the better option would be to have free time to engage in research and international activities. It would be lonely to have less opportunity to be directly involved with top students from international backgrounds, but I couldn't continue to do everything.

M. Aoki, *Transboundary Game of Life*,
https://doi.org/10.1007/978-981-13-2757-5_28

In terms of international activities, I have written four books in English and published in English the results of ten international projects that I have organized. This was not just a matter of inviting people to conferences, collecting the papers presented, and relying on the publisher. It required my all-out effort to choose the topics and compose the contents, select and negotiate with the authors of each chapter, organize the conference for discussions, edit the material for the conference volume, and gather the funding to make all this possible. I was fortunate to have co-editors, such as Professors Oliver Williamson, Ronald Dore, Hugh Patrick, and Yūjirō Hayami who worked with me. When I count all the researchers I worked with it comes to some 150 from seventeen countries. Sponsoring organizations include Japan's Ministry of Education, Suntory Foundation, the World Bank, the Swedish Collegium for Advanced Studies in Social Sciences, Stockholm School of Economics, International Economic Association, and RIETI.

The topics have been diverse encompassing corporations, financial systems, political economics, development economics, and corporate governance. In terms of policies, the World Bank Institute project "Corporate Governance in Transitional Economies" had a major impact. We posited that in the transformation from socialist planned economies to market economies, simply privatizing state-owned enterprises can precipitate the danger of "insider control" in which the corporate managers usurp state-owned assets.[1]

Publication of this volume was one of the reasons I was invited in 1994 to Beijing to attend a conference now known as "Jinglun Conference" (Chinese Economic System Reform International Discussion Conference) in an effort to secure the theoretical foundations of reform (Fig. 28.1). Arriving at the airport, I was welcomed by a woman who spoke Japanese with just a slight Chinese accent. She was the wife of Tatsuhito Tokuchi, who had been my student at Stanford some six years earlier. His father had been a military officer posted to New Guinea in prewar years. After the war's end, he vowed that Japan and China should never again go to war and visited China many times with his former military colleagues. Tokuchi went to China in 1964 with his parents where he experienced the Cultural Revolution. After graduating from Peking University, he was sent by Daiwa Securities where he was employed to study at Stanford. I had a hunch that he would play a major role in future economic relations between Japan and China. After he obtained his master's degree I urged him strongly to go to Wall Street and study the reality of an advanced stock market as it would help him in the future. He himself had intended to do so, and with the understanding of his company, after a few years' experience, he was now posted to China.

When we met again I mentioned that I was going to meet with Ms. Xiao Meng, the behind-the-scenes organizer of the Jinglun Conference, and he implored me to introduce him to her. I learned that her real name is Peng Xiaomeng, and that while she was at Peking University Middle School, her speech criticizing the reactionary

---

[1]The World Bank report on this project is contained in *Corporate Governance in Transitional Economies: Insider Control and Roles of Banks*, World Bank Institute, 1994.

For "corporate governance" issues in China, see Wu, Jinglian, *Gendai Chūgoku no Keizai kaikaku* (Economic reform in contemporary China), Chap. 5 "Kigyō kaikaku" (Corporate reform), NTT Shuppan: 2007.

Fig. 28.1 At Jinglun Conference (from left: Prof. Paul Milgrom, the author, Zhou Xiaochuan, later Governor of People's Bank of China)

educational system was lauded by Mao Tse-tung in his August 1966 "A Letter to the Red Guards," which raised in one fell swoop the status of the Red Guards movement.[2]

This meant she was one of the original Red Guards. But when the Red Guard movement changed character from its initial idealistic criticism of bureaucratism, and her group was denounced, it was a lone Japanese friend of Tokuchi who encouraged her to the end, waving a red flag from the roof of the school building.

Later, Tokuchi was invited to become Vice President of a subsidiary of the largest Chinese state-owned conglomerate China International Trust Investment Corporation, CITIC Securities, founded by Rong Yiren, known as "the Red Capitalist." Tokuchi led the growth of CITIC Securities to become a force greater than Nomura Securities. Speaking Mandarin with better pronunciation than the average Chinese, his reliable character has allowed him to establish a firm position in the core of China's economic circles. As to the true nature of Chinese economics, it is he that I now learn from.

The Jinglun Conference was held at the time when China was beginning its serious reforms on financial institution systems and corporate laws. It functioned under the leadership of the renowned reformist economist Professor Wu Jinglian and State Economic and Trade Commission deputy director Chen Qingtai, an architect of various economic reform measures of the time. Participating in this conference from abroad were corporate theory specialists like Paul Milgrom, Oliver Hart, and myself;

---

[2]"I enthusiastically support you. I also give enthusiastic support to the big-character poster of the Red Flag Combat Group of Peking University Middle School which said that it is right to rebel against the reactionaries; and to the very good revolutionary speech given by comrade P'eng Hsiao-meng representing their Red Flag Combat Group at the big meeting attended by all the teachers, students, administration and workers of Peking University on 25 July." Mao Tse-tung "A Letter to the Red Guards," August 1, 1966. *Long Live Mao Tse-tung Thought*, Red Guard publication.

and from China young brains behind Vice Premier Zhu Rongji: Zhou Xiaochuan, Lou Jiwei, and Guo Shuqing. Including this conference, I was able to meet three times with Premier Zhu Rongji. I was deeply impressed that he did not put on any airs, was a quick study on leading-edge economic theories, and was a leader who had the courage to push through unpopular policies if necessary to modernize the nation's economy. At that time, one draft proposal for reform of state-run corporations was the suggestion of a tiered governance structure. He listened attentively to our discussion that this rose from a planned economy-type thinking and would doubtless result in extreme inefficiency. Articles based on these discussions were published five years later in "Jinglun Conference Revisited" by Wu Jinglian.[3] This played a major role in forming the theoretical foundation for China's financial and corporate reforms. Now, Zhou Xiaochuan is Governor of People's Bank of China; Lou Jiwei is Chairman and CEO of China Investment Corporation, founded to manage China's massive foreign exchange reserves; and Guo Shuqing is Chairman of China Construction Bank, one of the largest commercial banks in China.

The person who worked behind the scenes on this conference and has kept up the personal network among the participants is Ms. Xiao Meng, the editor of "Comparative Studies," which has substantial influence in journalistic and academic spheres. As we share a similar life course of facing setbacks due to political participation in our youth, we have a comradely relationship regarding the comparative institutional analysis of China. She has clear judgments on what is good and bad and expresses her assessments of people without regard to self-interest, and there is much to learn from her powers of observation. But normally she is mild-mannered and sensitive in relating to people, and it is understandable that she is at the center of a wide network of persons of all ages. This is because her efforts arise not from economic or political power, or family connections, but from the intellectual strength that emanates from within her.

While in Morocco attending the International Economic Association World Congress, I had a tajine dinner at a restaurant overlooking the bazaar at Marrakesh with the Hungarian economist and then Association President Kornai and his family, when Ms. Xiao Meng came up in our conversation. Without much basis in fact, we likened the role of her intellectual network in economic reforms in China to the French ladies who ran the salons for intellectuals leading up to the French Revolution. She was eager to publish a Chinese version of Kornai's autobiography, but conditions in China did not permit this, so it is to be published in Hong Kong.

As I described in "Chap. 21: Visiting Closed China," my interest in China originated from my academic and intellectual curiosity to understand various types of societies. Later, while engaged in teaching and research at Stanford, I shared my academic interest in economics focusing on comparative institutional analysis and the transformation from planned economies to market economies with graduate students and researchers from China. In the past few years, many of them have returned to China and have begun to play a vital role in academic and economic areas. I have

---

[3] Wu, Jinglian et al., 1999, *Corporate Governance, Debt Restructuring and Bankruptcy Procedure: A Revisit to Jinglun Conference.*

also participated nearly every year since the Jinglun Conference in policy forums, conferences, and lectures at universities or research institutions related to the World Bank and the Chinese government.

Due to these connections, in 2003 I became one of the early foreigners who received the position of Adjunct Professor at Tsinghua University. The ceremony at that event was held in the very same room where, a quarter-century earlier during my trip to China, I had met for discussions with the head of the revolutionary committee acting as university president. I felt strongly that China had persisted on its long road for reform. But I also felt a deep satisfaction that I had continuously worked to observe and understand the society of this nation that could easily make a major reversal at any time.

As I have noted, my engagement with China did not start from an interest in the so-called "Japan–China friendship" movement; neither do I have among my current Chinese acquaintances hardly any of those who are related to that movement. But my encounters with various Chinese with whom I can candidly discuss common points of interest in intellectual, ideological, and policy matters have led to firm friendly relations. And that has helped in the launching of an innovative intellectual venture between Japan and China in 2005, when we faced a difficult time with the sudden eruption of anti-Japanese riots in China. The next chapter delves into this venture.

Chapter 29
Teaming up with Toyota on Environmental Issues

In July 2007, the Center for Industrial Development and Environmental Governance (CIDEG) at Tsinghua University in Beijing with the International Economic Association jointly sponsored an international round table conference with the title "Environmental Governance for Sustainable Development." Professor Geoffrey Heal of Columbia University and Professor Lawrence Goulder of Stanford University also participated in organizing this conference. In anticipation of the conference, CIDEG solicited papers for an essay contest on environmental economics from young Chinese economists under the age of 35. The winning essay was selected from thirty entrants and the winner gave a report in excellent English to the assembled world-class environmental scholars. Listening to the presentations, I had a strong sense of the rapid development of environmental economists in China from the younger generation.

The role of research institutes like CIDEG will no doubt increase in China, which is beset with serious problems of pollution that appear in the shadow of rapid economic growth. CIDEG was for me my sixth intellectual venture, launched jointly with Toyota Motor Corporation in October 2006. This effort began in summer 2004 when I became advisor to Toyota's social contribution activities. It appeared that Toyota wanted to hear a variety of opinions on what it could do in China as a corporate citizen (Fig. 29.1).

This was not the first time I had connected with Toyota. As I noted in "Chap. 23: Return to My Former Haunts," I had taken my students to visit the General Motors—Toyota joint venture NUMMI plant in the mid-1980s, at the height of American concern about trade friction in the automobile industry. Based on my observations, I created a model of the difference in the production methods between GM and Toyota as a gap in information systems. When my Stanford University colleague Prof. Milgrom, an authority on organizational theory, later went himself to see the Toyota plant in Kentucky, he told me, "Now that I have seen the plant, I understand the meaning of your model." It seems his background in working a summer job at a GM plant while in high school had helped him to understand the fundamental difference in work organization between Japan and the U.S. Even for

M. Aoki, *Transboundary Game of Life*,
https://doi.org/10.1007/978-981-13-2757-5_29

Fig. 29.1 At the inaugural reception for CIDEG: Toyota President Katsuaki Watanabe (center) and Tsinghua University Vice President Xie Jinghua (left), author (right)

theorists, on-site observation is important. Thus, it was extremely beneficial for me, as a company advisor, to regularly discuss political and economic topics with top Toyota management, learn about the market and technology of the automobile industry, and have opportunities to visit its closed plant in China.

I went to seek the advice of the economist Wu Jinglian and Chen Qingtai, Dean of School of Public Policy and Management, Tsinghua University, on what kind of social contribution activities would be most useful. Both of them were organizers of the Jinglun Conference in 1994, and since that time have been good discussion partners for me. Mr. Chen was the leader of Dongfeng Motor Corporation, one of the top three auto manufacturers in China, and now advocates the necessity for China's economy to shift course toward technologies to save its environment. Professor Wu's recommendations on Chinese economic reform consist of a high level of moral authority, and he became the first recipient of the China Economics Award.

What arose out of the discussions we three held were the Toyota Study Assistance Fund to support students who faced difficulty attending university for financial reasons and CIDEG. The Toyota Study Assistance Fund offers financial aid to twenty students from impoverished families to attend each of twenty local universities, totaling 400 student aid recipients. This fund is administered in an open way through the Soong Ching Ling Foundation. Among the high school teachers who enthusiastically recommend the educational advancement of students from poor families are quite a few former activists who were sent down to the countryside during the Cultural Revolution and remained to teach there. We have received moving letters from students who unexpectedly received financial assistance. The chairman of the Soong Ching Ling Foundation is Hu Qili, former member of the Politburo Standing Committee, said to have been the right-hand man of Hu Yaobang, General Secretary of the Communist Party. In his youth, he went to Prague and Moscow as the Chinese representative of the international students league, and had experience fighting the Soviet Union's "hegemony." The Japanese Zengakuren representative was his comrade in this struggle, and was a mutual friend. We shared our strong feelings in common of having lived through the same times.

Initially, Toyota contributed 400 million yen over five years to CIDEG as support for research on environmental economics and industrial research. It was agreed that Toyota would participate in board meetings along with Chinese leaders in environmental studies and other disciplines, but not be directly involved in the content of the research. Prof. Hu and I agreed to serve as joint chairs of the board of directors.[1]

Recently in China, there are intense conflicts among interest groups on such issues as environment, health care, and land expropriation. Universities can play a significant role as a place for calm discussion of these problems that are difficult to solve immediately through political means. On this point, the situation in China has become more and more like that in the U.S. The CIDEG board of directors includes the deans of Tsinghua University's Law School, School of Economics and Management, and School of Social Sciences, as well as the Chinese Academy of Sciences, famed for environmental technology. One of the purposes is to overcome the vertical separation between academic disciplines. An interdisciplinary approach is crucial to addressing environmental problems.

In addition to promoting individual research projects, CIDEG is also engaged in publication of translations of works such as Prof. Takahiro Fujimoto's *Nōryoku kōchiku kyōsō* (Capability building competition) (Chūkō Shinsho) and Michio Hashimoto's *Shishi kankyō gyōsei* (Personal history of environmental administration) (Asahi Shimbunsha). In a segment of Chinese policy makers, there is heightened awareness of the necessity to learn from Japan's experience in order to achieve sustained economic development. Prof. Fujimoto's book translated into Chinese caught the attention of the management of Chery Automobile, a private company, on the verge of making a rapid advance, which has led to an exchange with the Fujimoto research team at University of Tokyo. Frowning with disapproval that this sort of exchange will lead to technology drain will hinder continued progress in Japan's research and development. Put more broadly, it is essential that Japan increase its presence in a world of greater scarcity of environment and energy through its environmentally-conscious technological superiority and values.

Recently, several reports in international academic circles have indicated statistical results that stocks of companies that engage in contributions to society rise. How to interpret this finding was a topic of discussion at the international conference on environmental governance for sustainable development. If the common understanding that "the company is for the stockholders" is correct, putting profits toward societal contributions should lower stock values. This paradox questions basic issues: Who is the company for? What is the relationship between the company and society? It appears that it is not sufficient for a company just to engage with a particular market and achieve recognition from that source. A company can accumulate societal recognition from contributing to the sustainable use of the environment, a global "jointly

[1] For CIDEG, see http://www.cideg.tsinghua.edu.cn/column/Home.

owned land." In this age when the actual transfer of ownership is shifting from the corporate to the public sphere in terms of environmental rights, this becomes a type of insurance for the survival of the company and can lead to its increased valuation in the stock market.[2]

[2]For those interested, see my article "Linking Economic and Social Exchange Games: From Community Norm to CRS." https://siepr.stanford.edu/sites/default/files/publications/07-18_0.pdf.

Chapter 30
Social Game and Virtual Research Institute

As I write this memoir, I realize anew that my personal history is fully intertwined with contemporary history. Thus, when I receive comments from readers, such as "I was overcome with deep emotion that I live in contemporary times," or "I recalled my mother, a high school teacher, transcribing teaching materials late into the night," I feel we share something of our lives. As this was the first time I had written about the anti-Security Treaty struggles, those who knew my circumstances expressed concern, saying, "Are you all right having revealed so much?"; and those who didn't know said, "I'm stunned that you had such a radical past." However, I have no intention to talk about my behavior in those days by boasting about my exploits, and I expressed the reasons for not doing so in a frank manner (Chap. 10: Sugamo Prison and Anti-security Treaty Struggle). I was always conscious that in those days I was a log, if not a leaf, pushed along in the torrent of history. This made me maintain my silence about that time. In re-evaluating what the anti-Security Treaty struggle meant by thinking about it from the standpoint of a "social scientist," I came to feel that I wanted to impart my personal experiences of those days in a candid manner. An individual exists solely due to the world; and the world cannot exist without each individual's actions.

It may seem obvious and hardly worth mentioning at this late date, but in the past academic economics, sociology, and political science regarded either society or the individual as the primary actor and the other as secondary. Neoclassical economics and political science under its influence considered society to be composed of strong individuals with intrinsic beliefs and purposes. They thought that society was structured by the aggregate force of individuals' choices reflected in the market or elections; or (as in the case of Marxism as well) that society was dominated by the beliefs of the elite with its strong influence. In contrast to this, traditional sociology saw the existence of a dominant value system that took precedence over the individual which functioned as a way to cement individuals dispersed like grains of sand into a social structure. Each of these seems to reflect one facet of reality, but when we dig further, it can easily descend into a futile argument of which comes first, the chicken or the egg. Thus, if one commits to either academic field, it tended to make

M. Aoki, *Transboundary Game of Life*,
https://doi.org/10.1007/978-981-13-2757-5_30

dialogue impossible. My "wavering about economics" that I described in Chap. 20 came about from this stifling situation.

Under these conditions, the relationship between my personal history and the history of the times was a pressing issue for me personally and professionally. If the "strong individual" hypothesis of economics is true, the efforts of the Bund were a "failure"; and the change in my political beliefs afterward would be evidence of my "weakness." If I borrow the phrasing of my comrade in the Bund, Yasumasa Koga, what had been the prevailing thinking in pre-anti-Security Treaty times, "the perspective of skepticism about society and distrust of authority disappeared as if an evil spirit had been driven out by the anti-Security Treaty struggles"; and afterward it became an age in which one's "purpose in life" became the pursuit of a better material life.[1] If the long-standing sociological hypothesis of "the existence of society is a given" is correct, how can this sort of transformation in the dominant perspective on society be explained? Was the anti-Security Treaty struggle merely a meaningless much ado about nothing?

Setting the interpretation of my personal history aside, in recent years, it appears that there is a tendency among academic circles to re-think the cyclical mutual relationship between the individual and society or the times. I believe that the social science language which can be useful in understanding this comprehensive relationship between society and the individual can be expressed, as I have often noted, in the idea of a "game." Expressed in this way, I can imagine hearing voices stating, "Isn't game theory an outcome of economics which assumes the individual to be completely pragmatic? I'm tired of 'economic imperialism'"; or "Game theory is too abstract and separated from reality"; or even "Is it appropriate to treat society and people's lives as if they were in a game?"

However, in terms of the object of social science being "the mutual workings of people who choose their behavior by inferring other people's intention and behavior based on a set of rules," we can use the metaphor of a game. Here there is a decisive difference from physical phenomena whose object is determining the mutual workings between objectively existing physical elements. Therefore, the analogy of society as a game has already been proposed by several thinkers even before John von Neumann and Oskar Morgenstern proposed a mathematical game theory, and John Nash developed this further. We can cite, for example, Plato, David Hume, Adam Smith (as the moral philosopher before he became an economist), and the historian Johan Huizinga, who wrote *Homo Ludens: A study of the play element in culture* (1938).[2] These wise thinkers considered the rules for order in society to be created and maintained by people playing social games.

Why does the concept of games go beyond mere analogy and become useful in understanding the relationship between society and the individual? What can we

[1] Koga, Takamasa, "*Atogaki ni kaete*" (As an Afterword), *1954 Tōdai Komabaryō Shaken* (1954 University of Tokyo Komaba Dormitory Social Science Research Group).

[2] Plato, *Laws*, Volume 7; Hume, David, *A Treatise of Human Nature*; Smith, Adam, *The Theory of Moral Sentiments*; Huizinga, Johan, *Homo Ludens*.

learn from orthodox game theory? And how should this theoretical framework be expanded? I will state the essential points of my current thinking.

First, let me take up the issue of the general understanding that traditional game theory deals with financial motivation of individual agents, and therefore targeted economic behavior; thus, it is limited in its possibilities for application. It is true that human motives are diverse. But when we think about social games, we don't need to limit ourselves to considering only financial motives as people's aims. If the social relationship is one of a mutual aim of attaining a score that can be ranked, it becomes possible to use games as an analogy. This assessment can reflect in some cases an "altruistic" motive, or in other cases "civic-mindedness."[3]

With his comprehensive historical analysis, Huizinga, who proclaimed that rules based on play are the essence of order in human society, made the following deeply interesting point related to the purpose of play in society: "It is very curious how the words 'prize,' 'price' and 'praise' all derive more or less from the Latin pretium but develop in different directions."[4]

In the domain of economic exchange, everyone will pursue obtaining a high price. In the political domain, no matter how powerful, politicians cannot ignore people's opinions in exercising their power in such matters as taxation, conscription, punishment, income transfer, and supplying public goods. These opinions are expressed in various forms including winning or losing elections, unpopular policies, personality cults, and submission to or resistance against tyranny, with the ultimate outcome of the prize of obtaining, maintaining, or losing power. The mutually obtained praise gained through social exchange by the use of language and other social symbols to affect each other's feelings are intangible assets that are essential for us to live in society. Moreover, the games played in these various domains are inter-related. For example, even if a person can in the economic domain obtain a price by cheating others, if there is a certain prospect of receiving retaliation such as punishment (negative prize) or ostracism (negative praise), that person may think twice about engaging in such behavior. When we look at society in this way, it appears that game conditions are present in all domains of social life.

Second, by using game theory, we can bridge the divide of "which is first, the chicken or the egg" between economics thinking that "the individual makes society" (methodological individualism) and sociological thinking that "society makes the individual." Traditional game theory initially assumed that individuals had complete and accurate knowledge and prediction of the structure of the game and how the other side will behave, and that from this a perfect ability to calculate the optimal strategy would follow. However, this assumption has frequently been overturned by recent verifications by "experimental economics."[5] It can be said that people

[3]According to results of recent experimental economics, when the motive of experimental subjects is controlled for altruism, phenomena that could not be fully explained by past theories based on the hypothesis of selfish motives were better explained. See Kawagoe, Toshiji. *Jikken Keizaigaku* (Experimental Economics), Chap. 3, University of Tokyo Press, 2007.

[4]Huizinga, Johan. *Homo Ludens: A study of the play element in culture*, Beacon Press, 1955, p. 51 (First published: 1938; copyright: Roy Publishers, 1950).

[5]See Footnote 2.

play social games led by a common knowledge and shared belief, broad though it may be, that "social games are played this way by everyone." These can be written into enforceable laws, or an unspoken common understanding between workers and managers, as in the case of the life-time employment system that existed in Japan, or an intangible agreement such as social norms. Regardless of whether they like or agree ideologically with these rules, for all intents and purposes, people cannot ignore them. While these rules constrain the options in social play for each individual, at the same time for each individual who is not omniscient or omnipotent, they provide a guiding principle to select options for social play. Without these rules that have a dual nature, a stable society would not be able to exist.

What kind of rules, then, function effectively? No matter how well-written, a law on the books becomes a dead letter if the majority of people ignore it. An effective rule of the game is a basic pattern of behavior that everyone believes that, as others follow the rule, one would receive a penalty if one doesn't follow it. In addition, it is a pattern of behavior that everyone can reconfirm by everyone following the rule. For each individual, it looks like an exogenous restriction, but it is created and maintained by everyone together. This may seem a bit like a cryptic Zen dialogue, but this common knowledge for self-maintenance regarding basic patterns of behavior is termed "equilibrium" in game theory and can be conceptualized and analyzed. This is the recent approach of "institutions = social rules" of those engaged in comparative institutional analysis (CIA and noted in Chap. 25: Toward Comparative Institutional Analysis).[6]

Third, how, then, are the actual rules created in this equilibrium? It is easy to see that social norms are formed from the accumulation of experiences over generations. But what about formal, effective (non-arbitrary) rules, like laws? The philosopher John Rawls theorized that for a game to be played, rules must define a practice. He illustrated this with the example of baseball. If a batter in the batter's box is allowed to ask the umpire if he can get two more swings after two strikes, the game would not hold as the rules would not be applied.[7] In the past, economists handled the issue by stating that economic laws were defined by the political domain. What, then, defines the rules of the political game? Political scientists would say that they were defined by the constitution, which was the domain of legal scholars. Then, how are the rules of the constitutional system defined? When we push the limits of this argument, we fall into the dilemma of "infinite retreat." This is no longer the argument of whether the chicken or egg came first, but an infinite chain of evading accountability.

As a way of escaping this dilemma, the economist John McMillan discusses a sports example opposite to Rawls' idea. Football originated in the Middle Ages in various locations as a primitive game in which people were divided into two groups with the aim of getting a ball, which was a stuffed pig's bladder, to the opponent's end of the field. The number of players was not defined specifically, rules were made

[6]Aoki, Masahiko, *Hikaku seido bunseki ni mukete* (Toward Comparative Institutional Analysis), NTT Shuppan. The concept of "equilibrium of the totality" also plays a central role in the analysis of myths by Prof. Hayao Kawai, mentioned in Chap. 22: Thoughts on Corporations East and West.

[7]Rawls, John. "Two Concepts of Rules," *The Philosophical Review*, 64 (1955), pp. 3–32.

up in an ad hoc manner with no referees, and what was a rule in one village may not have been observed in the neighboring village. However, after a few hundred years, this folk football suddenly changed into a game with formal rules set in a top down fashion. McMillan states, "A typical market is born and grows like football."[8] The same can be said for the birth and growth of a nation as the entity that defines laws.

That is to say, a system with effective rules is not defined suddenly, or preceding the formation of a society, by a government, deity, or transcendental reasoning power. Rather, it is born from within the games played by people as the result of their joint behavior. As Huizinga noted, play creates social order, and constitutes the order itself.

What is the role of the individual in such a process in which people come up with rules in an evolutionary way through reciprocal interactions? Each individual, while using as a guideline the belief that others are following social rules, mobilizes his own particular knowledge, ability, and experience to recognize the problem, make efforts to solve it, and engages in actions. There may be times when a person consciously challenges the game by trying to change its rules. But at what times, and what kinds of challenges can produce results? Can that be accomplished by a single individual's efforts? Or, is it necessary to have a conscious or unconscious synchrony beforehand among people? Is there some sort of commonality that encourages the formation of rules for the social game and a common understanding which people are equipped with as a latent ability particular to them?

Even game theory, which thoroughly pursues the meaning of individual rationality, is moving toward the direction that there is some sort of pre-existing basic commonality among people's cognition that allows the establishment of social order ("equilibrium" in the game).[9] What might be called the common structure has, in the long history of human beings, been thought of as being formed by the "coevolution" of culture and genetics. Just as there are differences in individuals' genetics, this common structure is somewhat irregular. As the rules of the game gradually change, it appears that there is room for individual intention, effort, and ability to play a part. If social order can be formed by the workings of what is individual offsetting what is held in common, it may be said that the human image in terms of economics and the human image in terms of sociology should have been understood as complementary to each other from the start. Furthermore, contributions from evolutionary theory, cognitive science, neuroscience, and such become indispensable to this complementary structure.

What has come to light in cutting edge research on these issues in recent years transcending the various fields in social sciences and humanities is that there must be a relationality as yet not fully discovered between people's conscious and unconscious

[8]McMillan, John. *Reinventing the Bazaar: A Natural History of Markets*, W.W. Norton: 2002, pp. 12–13.

[9]For the latest game theory outcomes concluding that a stable game equilibrium may not come about unless there is a pre-existing prediction held in common, see Aumann, R. and A. Brandenburger, "Epistemic Conditions for Nash Equilibrium," *Econometrica* 63 (1995), pp. 1161–80. Also see Aoki, M., "Understanding Douglass North in Game-theoretic Language," http://papers.ssrn.com/sol3/papers.cfm?abstract_id=1083790.

cognitive structures and society's rules. Research and understanding of this scale cannot be achieved easily by individuals, even by those who have super-DNA like Galileo and Von Neumann.[10] Hence the need for super-interdisciplinary dialogue and development of a language that we have not had in the past.

To this end, I came to feel strongly that I wanted to discuss with and learn from scholars and students in varied fields about these issues. These feelings grew such that, incorrigibly, I have recently begun my seventh intellectual venture. Having been fortunate enough to become an honorary fellow at Tokyo Foundation, I started up an experimental project, the Virtual Center for Advanced Studies in Institution (VCASI). The aim was to create a virtual research institute in which scholars in the forefront of fields such as economics, sociology, political science, evolutionary theory, psychology, law, and regional studies could interact through the internet, transcending time and space. Their research topics would be the relationships among the various institutions of markets, organizations, nations, social norms. They would also include the connections between those institutions and individual cognitive structures. Of course, in order to effectively discuss these topics, it is essential that we have actual face-to-face meetings and informal conversations. However, there are many constraints to gathering scholars in these far-flung fields in a physical institute on a permanent basis, making this difficult. Therefore, this experimental approach is to provide a place for dialogue in cyberspace to supplement the dialogue in real time that is only possible on an occasional basis.

This virtual institute in cyberspace includes a coffee lounge where members can drop in for casual conversation; a seminar room for discussions based on papers written; and a library where members can read or download articles in specialized journals. Whether one is in one's own study or at an airport lobby, one can access this virtual institute in cyberspace. The steering committee that operates this institute meets weekly, even when I am in the U.S., by Skype. The meeting minutes are prepared during the meeting which all attendees can monitor, and immediately upon completion of the meeting are sent to the committee members. This prevents equivocation afterward, like "Did we decided on that?" The designing and improvement of this virtual institute's software through experimental learning is handled by young researchers led by Ken Suzuki, who was certified as a "super creator" by METI's Information-technology Promotion Agency.

As with a real research institute, this virtual institute must have an atmosphere allowing calm discussion. Thus, its use is limited for now to associated fellows. However, some of the research results are available on its public website.[11] In the future, we expect to open up the virtual institute to "friends of VCASI" in order to receive wide-ranging feedback from scholars and students interested in institutional research.

[10] John Von Neumann contributed to the mathematical foundation of quantum mechanics, played a leading role in the production of atomic bombs, designed the basis for current computer architecture (called the Von Neumann machine), and formulated the mathematical foundation for game theory as a social science theory.

[11] See http://www.vcasi.org/en.

It is as yet unclear how far this effort, heretofore impossible intellectual exchanges and products, will broaden under this format. This is the unfinished part of “my memoir” heading into the future.

Chapter 31
Conclusion: The Challenge of the Trans-boundary Game

From the perspective of each individual's subjective view, the fact that each individual is a player in the social game can be likened to each of them playing their own "game of life" within society. By participating in the social game, they reference, whether consciously or unconsciously, the way to play the game that is taken for granted in their world, in other words the "de facto rules of the game (systems)." However, as I have repeatedly stated, this is not the entirety of our experience. There are rich diversities and disparities in the images that people harbor about the forms of the social game. Individual factors, such as DNA and personal histories, affect the shaping of the image regarding the game, and the resultant awareness of the issues and inclinations for problem-solving. Also involved in the results of the selected actions are factors such as the local environment and occurrences surrounding the individual as well as chance, luck, and misfortune. Thus, the playing of the game of life contains "stories" inherent to each person.

In this piece on "My Memoir," I have written about the seven intellectual ventures that I have undertaken. If we look at them as parts of my game of life, some have been attempts to change the rules of the game (in the cases of the Bund; RIETI: Research Institute of Economy, Trade, and Industry); efforts to create new spaces for games to be played according to existing rules (in the cases of JJIE: *Journal of the Japanese and International Economies*; SJC: Stanford Japan Center; CIDEG: Center for Industrial Development and Environmental Guidance); and experiments in new ways of playing games (in the cases of CIA: Comparative Institutional Analysis; VCASI: Virtual Center for Advanced Studies in Institution). These efforts can be bundled together into my "trans-boundary game" as they attempted to go beyond the existing ways of the game's rules, places, and methods of play. What were the outcomes from playing these trans-boundary games? Did I win, or did I lose?

The attempts at the creation of a new international academic journal (JJIE), the establishment of a trans-border educational and research program for a university (SJC), and the founding of a research institution (CIDEG), while facing hurdles and hardships during their journeys, were enjoyable, and can be said to have landed on their original targets. There, they should be able to further their games according to

M. Aoki, *Transboundary Game of Life*,
https://doi.org/10.1007/978-981-13-2757-5_31

rather well-known rules. For the attempts to go beyond the boundaries of academic disciplines (CIA and VCASI), their destinations are not yet in sight; and as they are part of a major crossing of boundaries along with many others, I cannot say whether I have won or lost as an individual.

The results difficult to assess are the games in which I attempted to create new rules. The first such trans-boundary game I participated in, the effort of the Bund, seems to be regarded by many as a "defeat." As a social game, the halting of the revision of the U.S.–Japan Security Treaty, which was the aim of the Bund, was not accomplished; the far-reaching goal of the establishment of a revolutionary political party also ended in failure; and some may consider that these goals were misguided from the start. Yet, from the perspective of my game of life, I have a different view. As Takaaki Yoshimoto stated in the past, we were part of the "generation that attained an individualized character formation." (Chap. 3: Three of My Seniors) Entering the world of partial adulthood as we became university students, what awaited us was the world of the political game. But we were already prepared to express ourselves in a free and open-minded manner. We were naturally uncomfortable with the push to return politics to that before Japan lost the war, and we also felt out of place with the Communist Party that sought to manage mass movements in an authoritarian manner, riding on the myth of "the only non-convert that stuck to the anti-war position." Although we used the rhetoric of aiming to create a revolutionary party, for many in our generation, this was merely an expression of our intention to act on our own ideas within the domain of the political game.

As I described in "Chap. 10: Sugamo Prison and Anti-security Treaty Struggle," the anti-Security Treaty struggle changed the rules of the political game in ways that nearly all of the players had not intended. It would no longer be viable for those in power to make an effective play by exercising power while ignoring the democratic process, and the tradition-bound revolutionary party lost the possibility of being an effective game player. Furthermore, it put an end to the deification of Marxism that had long dominated the thinking of Japan's intellectuals. These changes were not what the Bund had intentionally anticipated or aimed for; rather, they were the opposite of its intentions. But the fact that the Bund, however unaware, acted as a catalyst to accelerate this change, and that it was able to do so, was no doubt because the times were already potentially headed that way. As I stated, the Bund as an organization was a device that intermediated the display of the initiative and autonomy of each individual. It would not be too farfetched to say that a new way of playing the game was germinating in that organization. Continuing to adhere to the old way of playing the game when the rules of the game have changed would mean following the fate of various leftist sects in the U.S. and Japan, eventually becoming extinct or taking the path of gradual disintegration and atrophy. (Chap. 12: Escape from the Front Lines; Chap. 18: Counterculture) Propelled by the current of the times, I withdrew from the old game and began searching out a new formulation for the game. Hence, I do not have a sense of victory, neither do I have a sense of defeat. Looking back, it might have been that this was an evolution in my game of life.

With RIETI I attempted to challenge the long-established rules of Japan's central governmental apparatus, but I was flung back by the wall of rules of the old game and I retired from the game. (Chap. 26: To Kasumigaseki; Chap. 27: Light and Shadow of Independent Administrative Institutions) This experience allowed me to better understand the workings of the rules of long-established games. Since then I have had several offers to participate in policy research institutes, but I had no intention of repeatedly playing games with old rules. This is because I think that the awareness that those rules will not pertain forever will quietly permeate throughout society.

Reviewing my ventures in this way, I see that each trans-boundary game is inextricably related to the others, forming a seamless series as a whole. It may appear to be self-rationalization with the advantage of hindsight, but I come to the conclusion that as long as I live there is no end to my game of life, and no victory or defeat. Or, perhaps I should say victory and defeat alternate "like the strands of a rope." If it were settled either way, there would be no point to living. This is where I find the fun and gravity in the game of life.

Bibliography

Anderson, B. (1998). *The spectre of comparisons: Nationalism, Southeast Asia and the World*. New York: Verso.

Aoki, M. (1960). Review of international communist movements. *Puroretaria tsūshin* (Proletarian bulletin) No. 6 (December). In S. Shima (Ed.), (1992) *Bunto no shisō 4* (Ideology of the Bund 4). Tokyo: Hihyōsha.

Aoki, M. (1971a). *Soshiki to keikaku no keizai riron* (*Economic theory of organization and planning*). Tokyo: Iwanami Shoten.

Aoki, M. (1971b). Two planning processes for an economy with production externalities. *International Economic Review, 12*, 403–414.

Aoki, M. (1988). *Information, incentives, and bargaining in the Japanese economy*. Cambridge, UK: Cambridge University Press.

Aoki, M. (1984). *The co-operative game theory of the firm*. Oxford University Press.

Aoki, M. (1995). *Keizai system no shinka to tagensei* (*The evolution and diversity of economic systems*). Tokyo: Toyo Keizai Shinpōsha.

Aoki, M. (2001a). *Information, corporate governance and institutional diversity*. Oxford University Press.

Aoki, M. (2001b). *Toward a comparative institutional analysis*. Cambridge: MIT Press.

Aoki, M. (2002). *Utsuriyuku kono jūnen: ugokanu shiten* (*Unwavering coordinates in a decade of flux*). Tokyo: Nihon Keizai Shinbunsya.

Aoki, M. (2003). *Hikaku seido bunseki ni mukete* (*Toward comparative institutional analysis*). Tokyo: NTT Shuppan.

Aoki, M. (2008). *Understanding Douglass North in the game-theoretic language*. http://papers.ssrn.com/sol3/papers.cfm?abstract_id=1083790.

Aoki, M., & Andō, H. (2002). *Modularity: Atarashii sangyo architecture no honshitsu* (*Modularity: A new industrial architecture*). Economic Policy Review Series. Tokyo: Tōyō Keizai Shinpōsha.

Aoki, M., & Dore, R. (Eds.). (1994). *The Japanese firm: Sources of competitive strength*. Oxford University Press.

Aoki, M., & Tsuru, K. (2004). Keizai seisaku bunseki series (*Economic policy analysis series: fiscal reforms of Japan: Redesigning the frame of the state*). Tokyo: Tōyō Keizai Shinpōsha.

Aoki, M., Kim, H., & World Bank. (1995). *Corporate governance in transitional economies: Insider control and roles of banks*. Washington, D.C.: The World Bank.

Aoki, M., Sawa, A., & Daidō, M. (Eds.). (2001). *Daigaku kaikaku: kadai to soten* (*University reform: Topics and arguments*). Tokyo: Tōyō Keizai Shinpōsha.

M. Aoki, *Transboundary Game of Life*,
https://doi.org/10.1007/978-981-13-2757-5

Arrow, K. J., & Hurwicz, L. (1960). Decentralization and computation in resource allocation. In R. W. Pfouts (Ed.), *Essays in economics and econometrics*. Chapel Hill, NC: University of North Carolina Press.

Asanuma, B. (author); Tatsuya Kikutani (ed.) (1998) *Nihon no kigyō soshiki: kakushinteki tekiō no mekanizumu* (*Organization of Japanese firms: Mechanism for innovative adaption*). Tokyo: Tōyōkeizai Shinpōsha.

Aumann, R., & Brandenburger, A. (1995). Epistemic conditions for Nash equilibrium. *Econometrica, 63,* 1161–1180.

Fujisawa, N. (2000–2001). *Fujisawa Norio chosaku shū* (*Collected works of Norio Fujiwawa*). Tokyo: Iwanami Shoten.

Hirasawa, F. (2000). *Sengokubune Mukunoura* (*Cargo ships in Mukunoura*). Hiroshima: Innoshima City Bunkazai Kyokai.

Huizinga, J. (1938). *Homo Ludens: Proeve Ener Bepaling Van Het Spelelement Der Cultuur;* 1955. *Homo Ludens: A study of the play element in culture*. Beacon Press.

Hume, D. (1738). *A treatise of human nature*.

Innoshima Shi shi Hensyu Committee. (Ed.). (1968). *Innoshima Shi shi* (*Innoshima City history*). Hiroshima: Innoshima shi shi Hensyu Committee.

Kawagoe, T. (2007). *Jikken keizaigaku* (*Experimental economics*). Tokyo: University of Tokyo Press.

Kawai, H. (1967). *Yungu shinrigaku nyūmon* (*Introduction to Jungian psychology*). Tokyo: Baifūkan.

Kesey, K. (1962). *One flew over the Cuckoo's nest*. New York: Viking Press.

Koga, T. (1954). Atogaki ni kaete (As an Afterword). In *1954 Tōdai Komabaryō Shaken* (1954 University of Tokyo Komaba Dormitory Social Science Research Group).

Koga, Y. et al. (Eds.). (1994). *Tōdai Komabaryō Shaken* (1994 University of Tokyo Komaba Dormitory Social Science Research Group). Tokyo: Tōdai Komabaryō Shaken Kankokai.

Maeda, Y. (2008). *Suisen toire no sangyōshi: nijūseiki Nihon no miezaru inobēshon* (*Industrial history of the flush toilet: Invisible innovations in twentieth century Japan*). Nagoya: Nagoya University Press.

Mao, T. (1966). A letter to the Red Guards, August 1. *Long live Mao Tse-tung thought*. Red Guard Publication.

Matsumoto, S. (1974–1975). *Shanghai jidai* (Shanghai times). Tokyo: Chūō Kōron Shinsha.

McMillan, J. (2002). *Reinventing the bazaar: A natural history of markets*. New York: W.W. Norton.

Milgrom, P., & Roberts, J. (1992). *Economics, organization and management*. NJ: Prentice Hall.

Nishibe, M. (1975). *Socio economics (Socioeconomics)*. Tokyo: Chūō Kōron Shinsha.

Noguchi, T. (1968). *Mishima Yukio no sekai* (*The world of Yukio Mishima*). Tokyo: Kōdansha.

Ōtake, H. (2007). *Shinsayoku no Isan: New Left kara Post Modern e* (*Heritage of the New Left: From the New Left to Post Modern*). Tokyo: University of Tokyo Press.

Rawls, J. (1955). Two concepts of rules. *The Philosophical Review, 64,* 3–32.

Rawls, J. (1971). *A theory of justice*. CO: Belknap.

Samuelson, P. A. (1947) *Foundations of economic analysis*. Harvard University Press.

Searle, J. R. (2005). What is an institution? *Journal of Institutional Economics, 1*(1), 2.

Shima, S. (1992). Bunto shishi (zenhen) (Personal history of the Bund–1). In Shima, Shigeo (Ed.) *Bunto no shisō 1* (*Ideology of the Bund 1*). Tokyo: Hihyōsha.

Shima, S., & Takazawa, K. (Eds.). (1992). *Bunto no shisō* (Ideology of the Bund): *Vol. 1 Kyōsanshugi* (*Communism*); *Vol. 4 Puroretaria tsūshin* (*Proletarian Bulletin*). Tokyo: Hihyōsha.

Shimizu, I. (1972) *Rinrigaku note* (*Notes on ethics*). Tokyo: Iwanami Shoten.

Shimizu, M. (2007). *Keizai zaisei senki*. Nihon Keizai shinbun shuppan. Tokyo.

Smith, A. (1759). *The theory of moral sentiments*.

Suzumura, K. (2005). An interview with Paul Samuelson: Welfare economics, 'old' and 'new', and social choice theory. *Social Choice and Welfare, 25,* 327–356.

Wu, J. (2007). *Gendai Chūgoku no keizai kaikaku* (*Economic reform in contemporary China*). Tokyo: NTT Shuppan.

Yamaguchi, I. (1958). Jūgatsu kakumei no michi to wareware no michi: kokusai kyōsanshugi undō no rekishiteki kyōkun (The road of the October Revolution and our road: historical lessons from the international communist movement). *Nihon Kyōsantō Tōdai Saibō Kikanshi: Marukusu Rēnin shugi* (Japan Communist Party University of Tokyo Cell Bulletin: Marxism-Leninism) No. 9.

Yoshimoto, T. (1960). Sengo sedai no seiji shisō (Political ideology of the postwar generation). In *Itan to seikei* (*Heterodoxy and orthodoxy*). Tokyo: Gendai Shichōsha.

Yoshimoto, T. (1971). *Gendai shi techō rinzō: Yoshimoto Takaaki* (*Modern poetry notebook special supplement: Takaaki Yoshimoto*). Tokyo: Shichōsha.

Name Index

M. Aoki, *Transboundary Game of Life*,
https://doi.org/10.1007/978-981-13-2757-5

MIX
Papier aus verantwortungsvollen Quellen
Paper from responsible sources
FSC® C105338

If you have any concerns about our products,
you can contact us on
ProductSafety@springernature.com

In case Publisher is established outside the EU,
the EU authorized representative is:
Springer Nature Customer Service Center GmbH
Europaplatz 3, 69115 Heidelberg, Germany

Printed by Libri Plureos GmbH
in Hamburg, Germany